ON FOOT FROM COAST TO COAST

ON FOOT FROM COAST TO COAST

The North of England Way

DAVID MAUGHAN

MICHAEL JOSEPH

LONDON

MICHAEL JOSEPH LTD

Published by the Penguin Group
27 Wrights Lane, London w8 5tz
Viking Penguin Inc., 375 Hudson Street, New York, New York 10014, USA
Penguin Books Australia Ltd, Ringwood, Victoria, Australia
Penguin Books Canada Ltd, 10 Alcorn Avenue, Toronto, Ontario, Canada m4v 3b2
Penguin Books (NZ) Ltd, 182–190 Wairau Road, Auckland 10, New Zealand

Penguin Books Ltd, Registered Offices: Harmondsworth, Middlesex, England

First published 1997
1 3 5 7 9 10 8 6 4 2

Set in 10.5/12pt Monotype Perpetua
Designed in QuarkXpress 3.3 on an Apple Macintosh
Printed in England by Clays Ltd, St Ives plc

A CIP catalogue record for this book is available from the British Library

ISBN 0 7181 4151 2

The moral right of the author has been asserted

CONTENTS

ACKNOWLEDGEMENTS

I should like to thank my mother and father who introduced me to the pleasures of walking at a very early age. Alfred Wainwright, to whom this book is dedicated, inspired me through his writings to devise my own coast to coast walk. I am grateful to my editor (also AW's), Jenny Dereham, for giving me the opportunity to publish this book. Her extensive experience and knowledge has been invaluable, while her attention to detail, enthusiasm and efficiency have contributed greatly to the completion of the book. I also wish to thank Chris Jesty for having patiently re-drawn my maps, making many improvements.

I would particularly like to thank the friends who have joined me on walks — Ged Murray, Andy Lovett, Derek Bryanton, Andrew Cochrane and Bob Kersey — as well as other walkers and outdoor enthusiasts I have met; their companionship, conversation and humour have added greatly to the joys of walking.

Special mention needs to be made of Adrian Verity who, whilst Chairman of the University of York Outdoor Society, checked the route and in doing so became the first person, after the author, to complete the 200-mile walk. Thanks to the Youth Hostels Association and to Steve Johnson and Andrew Pannett at The University of York for their advice and assistance. Also to Bob Dicker of the National Trust who helped in planning the detour to the Bridestones Nature Reserve. I also wish to acknowledge the use of Alfred Wainwright quotations in the introduction to this book: © 1992 Michael Joseph Ltd. Every effort has been made, without success, to contact Anne Daniet to obtain permission for use of the Paradise poem.

Finally, I would like to thank my wife Celia, my son Alastair and my daughter Sophie without whose support the book would not have been possible.

INTRODUCTION

My first taste of the attraction of long-distance walking was when I completed the Dales Way in Spring 1990. This was a preparatory walk for Wainwright's Coast to Coast Walk which I did the following year, in early April. I enjoyed Wainwright's walk immensely and I have no doubt that the 'master fellwalker' selected one of the finest, if not the finest, long-distance routes in England. I anticipated doing the walk again sometime in the future, but I was a little concerned at its increasing popularity; this was borne out when, later that year, I met some Coast to Coast walkers completing the walk for the third year in succession.

One evening, when I was mulling over Wainwright's Pictorial Guide, I read his Personal Notes in Conclusion at the end of the book. I had read them before, of course, but on this occasion my eyes stopped in the middle of page xiv: '. . . but I would feel I had succeeded better in arousing interest for the planning of private long-distance walks if the book induced some readers to follow instead their own star and find their own rainbow's end'. Wainwright succeeded in my case and there and then I decided to take up his challenge to plan my own alternative coast to coast walk which I hoped would be as equally attractive as Wainwright's and which would allow a relatively solitary walk across England, taking in three of the country's finest National Parks – the Lake District, the Yorkshire Dales and the North York Moors.

It was with a little trepidation that I arrived at a wet Ravenglass station on 29 March 1993 to embark on this long-awaited adventure – my own coast to coast walk. Three months earlier I was in York District Hospital's casualty department having strained knee ligaments in the Boxing Day Dads' football match held annually in my local village. I was uncertain now whether my knee would withstand 200 miles of walking across England. I also wondered whether my coast to coast route would meet all the original objectives I had set, the overriding objective of which was to select the best southerly coast to coast route.

I was not to be disappointed and, indeed, with excellent weather for most of the fourteen-day walk, all my expectations were exceeded.

The route I devised goes through the best countryside in the southern Lake District and includes the secluded and beautiful Esk and Duddon valleys. There are views of many majestic mountains, including Scafell and the Old Man of Coniston, and the energetic can include walks to these summits if time allows. Wordsworth wrote a series of thirty-five poems on the theme of Duddon and described the 'majestic Duddon' making a 'radiant progress towards the deep'; the River Duddon is one of twenty-one delightful rivers seen on the walk. The route skirts magnificent lakes including Coniston Water and Windermere as well as passing Tarn Hows.

After leaving Windermere Youth Hostel and passing through the delightful Troutbeck valley, the viewpoint of Orrest Head is reached. In 1930 Alfred Wainwright, at the age of twenty-three, came to the Lake District for the first time and on the first day of his holiday climbed from Windermere to Orrest Head. It was a moment that changed his life as, arriving at the little summit, he 'beheld a magnificent view. It was a moment of magic, a revelation so unexpected that I stood transfixed, unable to believe my eyes . . . This was truth. God was in Heaven that day and I a humble worshipper.'

From Orrest Head, Windermere the lake can be seen in its entire length. There are also views to the Langdale Pikes, the Coniston Fells, Bowfell, the Crinkle Crags and the great Scafell range. Windermere is nearly eleven miles long, and is England's longest lake.

Leaving Windermere (the town), the walk follows the route of the Dales Way to enter the Yorkshire Dales by lovely Dentdale. After crossing the scenic Settle–Carlisle railway line, the 'Three Peaks' (Pen-y-ghent, Ingleborough and Whernside) are skirted, and the Pennine Way is then followed into broad Wensleydale. The route includes the spectacular waterfalls of Hardraw Force and Aysgarth Falls and one of the Dales' largest expanses of water, Semer Water. Historical attractions abound in Wensleydale, including a Roman fort at Bainbridge, the massive ruins of Bolton Castle and the Norman castle at Middleham. The walk also visits Jervaulx Abbey before the long crossing of the north-ern end of the Vale of York to reach Thirsk, famous for its racecourse and James Herriot.

Soon the White Horse of Kilburn on the Hambleton Hills escarp-ment comes into view, with a climb up onto Sutton Bank from where there are magnificent views. The route briefly follows the Cleveland Way to Helmsley (with a short detour to visit Rievaulx Abbey) and thence to the beautiful, but often barren, North York Moors. The route proceeds both through quiet valleys and over fine open moorland to the picturesque village of Hutton-le-Hole with, situated in the cen-tre, the Ryedale Folk Museum. Between the quiet villages of Lasting-ham and Levisham, the North Yorkshire Moors Railway is crossed at Levisham station. Walkers with time to spare should not miss the opportunity to take a train, often steam, to Goathland or Grosmont; the scenery from the train is spectacular.

The route soon enters the Hole of Horcum where the moor falls away 400 feet into a vast hollow. After ascending from the Hole and admiring dramatic retrospective views, a delightful detour to the National Trust's Bridestones Nature Reserve can be included to see unusual rock formations. Pleasant country and forest walking is includ-ed on the final stretch to Scarborough and the walk is completed by dipping one's feet in the North Sea at Scarborough's North Bay – and I am not ashamed of borrowing this habit from Wainwright's walkers up the coast at Robin Hood's Bay.

Unlike AW, as he is affectionately known, I am not a solitary walker and, for me, coast to coast adventures are to be shared with true-lasting friends as well as fellow walkers *en route*. I think long-distance walks are for all age groups, and I owe a debt of gratitude to the Youth Hostels Association which welcomes walkers of all ages and, very often, of limited means. To repay this debt, I have deliberately tried to link the route to existing youth hostels. The Association introduces children and young people to the outdoor world in a unique way; it also enables 'aged' fathers and mothers to share outdoor experiences and adventures with their own children, young people and others. For help and advice with booking Youth Hostels along the route, contact YHA, PO Box 11, Matlock, Derbyshire DE4 2XA, or telephone 01629 825850.

All the youth hostels, apart from Ellingstring and Lockton, provide full catering provision of breakfast, packed lunch and dinner. A small shop is available at Ellingstring whilst an inn provides evening meals at Levisham, one mile from Lockton Youth Hostel. Walkers should note that Scarborough Youth Hostel is just over a mile from the end of the walk. Although there are no youth hostels at Ravenglass, Burneside (although Kendal Youth Hostel is nearby), Sedbergh, Thirsk or Hutton-le-Hole, they do have a wide range of accommodation such as bed and breakfast establishments and hotels. Further information is available from the relevant Tourist Information Centres.

Ravenglass beach is the start or end of the walk depending on whether you are crossing England from west to east or east to west. In order to have prevailing weather on your back, I recommend the west to east direction, as Wainwright did for his Coast to Coast Walk. The route keeps to rights of way, permissive paths or established paths, tracks or roads throughout. Some paths to viewpoints are obvious through use on the ground, albeit not always on the map. The countryside changes with surprising speed and landmarks, particularly stiles and gates, disappear, are moved or replaced in a different form. Since signposts frequently disappear, I do not rely on them except where there is little else to direct you. Every effort has been taken to ensure that the book is as up-to-date as possible at the time of publication and the route has been 'tested' as recently as possible.

Ravenglass is on the scenic coastal railway line between Carlisle, Barrow-in-Furness and Lancaster and has connections to the London to Glasgow Inter-City line and is therefore accessible from all parts of the country. It is recommended that walkers arrive the day before starting the walk in order to spend time a little time enjoying this quiet coastal area of Lakeland; an interesting and restful ride on the Ravenglass and Eskdale Railway should be included if time allows.

Scarborough has a main line railway station which has connections to the London to Edinburgh Inter-City line and provides an easy return journey to all parts of the country. An overnight stay in Scarborough is recommended in order to 'celebrate' a fine achievement in completing the coast to coast walk.

At the beginning of each Day or section of the walk, there is a summary of what lies ahead which will help walkers to plan their day and decide which places of interest they want to visit and how much time they can afford to spend at each. The mileage given for detours is the distance there and back. Facilities available along the route are also listed, such as accommodation, post offices, bus services, shops and hotels/inns. Bus services can change and, particularly in remote locations, are often infrequent and you are recommended to check schedules prior to using them. There are few banks on the way and you might therefore decide to have some money in a post office account to cover everyday expenses. Most accommodation, particularly youth hostels, can be paid for by cheque or, less frequently, credit card.

Remember that this walk is not meant to be a challenge to see how fast you can walk from Ravenglass to Scarborough. It is a walk to be enjoyed and to encourage your interest in the wonderful English countryside and places of interest to see or visit. The daily recommended mileage in the guide takes account of the varying terrain and points of interest *en route*.

For those who embark on a coast to coast adventure the spiritual and physical rewards are beyond description. I hope you accept the challenge and discover the best of England's countryside.

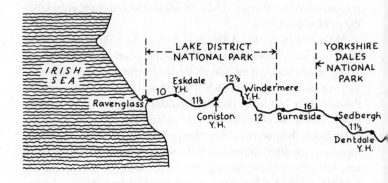

ORDNANCE SURVEY MAPS REQUIRED
in order of use to the scale of 1:25,000

Outdoor Leisure

   6 The English Lakes, South Western area
   7 The English Lakes, South Eastern area
  19 Howgill Fells and Upper Eden Valley
   2 Yorkshire Dales, Western area
  30 Yorkshire Dales, Northern & Central areas

Pathfinder

630 Middleham & Jervaulx Abbey
631 Bedale & Pickhill
641 Ripon
621 Thirsk

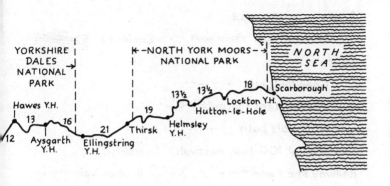

Outdoor Leisure

26 North York Moors, Western area
27 North York Moors, Eastern area

Although the Outdoor Leisure and Pathfinder maps can be replaced by
1:50,000 Landranger maps, less detail is then provided so the former
are certainly recommended. However, the 1:50,000 Landranger maps
in order of use are: 96, 97, 90, 98, 99, 100, 101.

THE ROUTE GUIDE: SYMBOLS AND ABBREVIATIONS

Route on public road

    Unenclosed ≈≈≈≈≈   Enclosed ⌇⌇⌇ wall / fence/hedge

Route

    Good footpath - - - - - - -

    Intermittent footpath ·-·-·—-·-

    No visible path ··············

Contours at 100-foot intervals ····1000'···· / ····1100'····

Railway line ▬▭▬▭▬   Broken wall ∘∘∘∘∘∘∘∘

Trees ⚇⚇⚇   Marshy ground ⸓⸓⸓   Crags ⋯⋯ ⋯⋯

Buildings ▰▰   Youth Hostel ▲   Church ⚲

Summit cairn △   Other cairn △   Viewpoint ☀

Stream or river ⟶   O.S. column ▱
    (Arrow indicates direction of flow)

Waterfalls ⟶⟶   Bridge ⟫⟪

Map continuation (indicates page number) ⊣ 50

Miles from Ravenglass ⟨40⟩

Abbreviations:

ɢ gate   ꜱ stile   Y.H. Youth Hostel

Approximate map scale: 2½ inches to the mile.
North is always at the top of the page.

Ravenglass to Eskdale Youth Hostel

Distance: 10 miles (11 miles including the detour to Dalegarth Force)
Going: Easy
Highest point: Muncaster Fell – 688 feet
Map required: O. S. Outdoor Leisure 6 English Lakes, South
Western area

The vertical exaggeration of this and all succeeding diagrams is x 4.

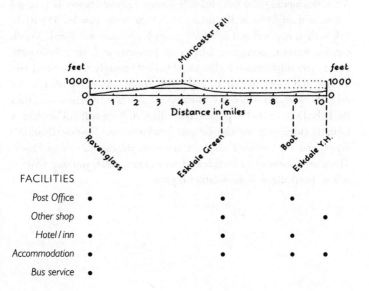

The first day's walking is to be savoured and, since it is only ten miles, there is time for some of the following: see a Roman bath house, visit the medieval Muncaster Castle, climb to a superb viewpoint at Hooker Crag, see the passing trains of the Ravenglass and Eskdale Railway and find the secluded Dalegarth Force which is situated in an enchanting wooded gorge.

The start of the walk is on the beach at Ravenglass and before setting out it is essential to dip a toe into the tidal estuary of the Irish Sea. After leaving the beach and passing the Roman Bath House, you soon arrive at Muncaster Castle where there is an opportunity to explore the castle and its delightful grounds, which include an owl centre. As you proceed from the castle over the undulating Muncaster Fell, there are magnificent views ahead, particularly from Hooker Crag, of the Scafell range of mountains and the delightful Eskdale and Miterdale valleys. After descending the fell, Eskdale Green railway station is reached where you might be lucky and see one of the trains pass by. The River Esk is then reached and followed through pleasant woodland. Watch out for herons, peregrine falcons or buzzards and, near Dalegarth Force, you might catch a glimpse of deer. I strongly recommend you include the short detour to Dalegarth Force, especially after heavy rain; the gorge in which it is situated is more like the Himalayas than the Lake District. In the picturesque village of Boot visit St Catherine's Church (look out for the famous headstone on Thomas Dobson's grave) and the restored 13th-century cornmill can also be included. There are a number of local hostelries *en route* which you may wish to call at, particularly if the weather is poor.

Ravenglass

Ravenglass consists only of a main street along the seafront, this road descending to the tidal estuary of the rivers Mite, Irt and Esk. Its main claim to fame is as the western home of the Ravenglass and Eskdale Railway, England's oldest narrow-gauge railway. At Ravenglass station there is a small railway museum which displays models, photographs and railway relics, while the former British Rail station has been turned into a pub called the Ratty Arms. In 1875 Whitehaven Iron Mines Ltd built a 3-ft gauge railway from the station at Ravenglass to the Nab Gill Mines at Boot about seven miles up the valley. A year later it was opened to passengers. It survived the failure of the mining company in 1882 but closed in 1913. Two years later it was reopened with a 15-inch gauge and a terminus at Dalegarth just short of Boot. It continued to carry passengers and freight, including granite from Beckfoot quarry, off and on until 1960. Then, when it seemed the end had come, the railway was put up for auction and purchased, with help from Colin Gilbert and Lord Wakefield of Kendal, by a preservation society for £12,000. Each year thousands of visitors travel on the railway now known as 'La'al Ratty' (the local dialect for 'little'). There are several steam engines in use. The railway and museum are open daily.

The Romans made Ravenglass their naval base for the whole of their occupation of north-west England. A recent find on the beach was a Roman diploma, this being sent from Rome during their occupation of Britain between AD 43 and 410 and representing a soldier's discharge paper awarding him Roman citizenship. The Bath House, known as Walls Castle (near Walls Mansion), is one of the highest standing remains of a Roman building in this country and is all that remains of their fort Glannaventa. Ravenglass received its market charter in 1208, one of the first in what is now Cumbria.

Leaving the beach, head south, turning left away from the river, and pass under the railway bridge. Turn right and the path leads towards the ruins of the Roman bath house. Turn left before Walls Mansion and follow the drive to Newtown. Go through the gate on your left, keeping left of the enclosed grounds. Ascend through a small new plantation to a step-stile in a fence. Follow the sketchy path to a gateway in an old fence (not marked on the map). Head north-east across open parkland to a wall and a gate and enter the grounds of Muncaster Castle.

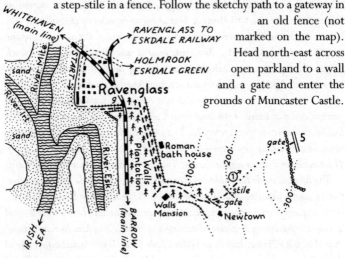

[*see* map opposite] Follow the path ahead through trees, ignoring a narrow, faint path off to your left. Turn left down a stony track and then immediately turn right to follow a series of footpath signs which guide you across a lawn.

Muncaster Castle

In this enormous granite and sandstone structure are beautiful tapestries, furniture and paintings. In 1464, Henry VI hid here and, in gratitude, presented the lovely glass 'Luck of Muncaster' bowl to Sir John Pennington; a replica is on view. It is said that as long as it remains intact the Penningtons will live and thrive

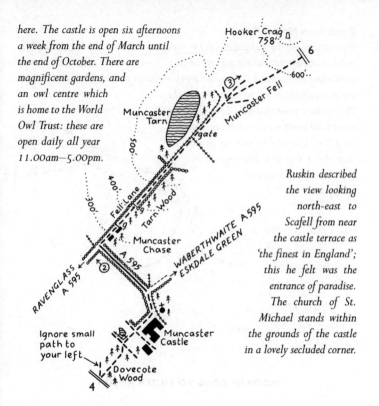

here. The castle is open six afternoons a week from the end of March until the end of October. There are magnificent gardens, and an owl centre which is home to the World Owl Trust: these are open daily all year 11.00am–5.00pm.

Ruskin described the view looking north-east to Scafell from near the castle terrace as 'the finest in England'; this he felt was the entrance of paradise. The church of St. Michael stands within the grounds of the castle in a lovely secluded corner.

MUNCASTER CASTLE TO HOOKER CRAG

Follow the drive ahead and uphill to pass the church on your right and shortly turn left onto the main, but not very main A595. At a sharp corner in the road, take the wide track on your right; this is named Fell Lane on the O.S. map. The track ascends through two gates and past Muncaster Tarn, hidden in trees, at a third gate. Continue straight on, ignoring all paths to the right and left. Hooker Crag will shortly be above you on the left. The main route skirts to the right of the crag.

Deviation to Hooker Crag

A deviation (for the viewpoint only) is highly recommended by taking the left-hand ascending path to the top of the crag. From the O. S. column on Hooker Crag, there are excellent views to the north of Scafell and the Illgill Head ridge, and a retrospective view to Ravenglass in the west.

The nuclear power station, Sellafield, can be seen to the north-west and, on a clear day, the Isle of Man can be seen out to sea. From the O. S. column bear right and descend to rejoin the main path.

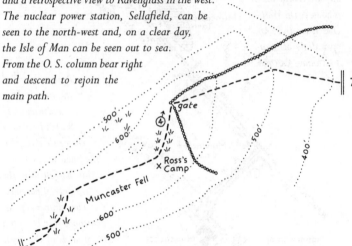

HOOKER CRAG TO SILVER KNOTT

Continue along the main path which skirts a marsh and soon passes Ross's Camp on your right. The stones were put together by members of a Victorian shooting party who raised the massive flat slab onto the other stones to serve as a luncheon table. The top of the slab is inscribed ROSS'S CAMP 1883. Little is known about Ross other than that he was an agent for the Muncaster estate around this time. The path descends to more marshy ground and then goes through a gate in the wall. There are superb views ahead north-east to Miterdale, Illgill Head and Scafell. The path now begins to skirt Silver Knott on its right flank.

A cairn on top of Silver Knott is a few yards to the right of the TV signal receiver. The path starts to descend to a gate in the wall. Go through the gate and follow the descending path. Soon after some gorse bushes, at a track, go right through a gate and immediately left to walk across rough pasture, passing to the left of a prominent upthrust of rocks and trees. Go through a broken fence (not shown on the map), and keep to the left of a large field. Then, by skirting some gorse bushes, head to the corner of the field to go through a stile by a gate and follow an enclosed bridleway. Walk past the entrance to Eskdale Green's station and turn right at the road. Continue on along the road shortly to reach the King George IV Inn.

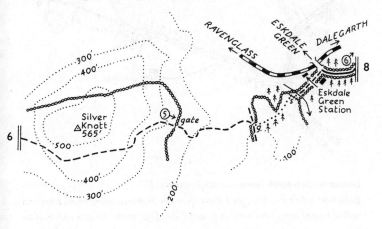

Having passed the inn, head down the road to Forge Bridge which crosses the River Esk. The Esk rises as a mountain stream in the heart of England's highest mountains, the Scafell group. It descends from around 2,400 feet to only 400 feet in a mere five miles, and remains throughout the journey clear and sparkling. Cross the bridge and turn left soon to go over a stile. Head slightly away from the river until a gate is reached, shortly followed by another gate near a barn. Walk past the barn and go through three more gates.

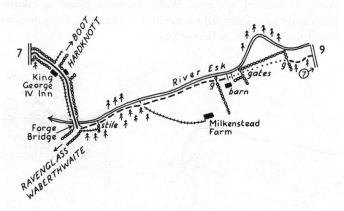

Detour to Dalegarth Force [*see* map opposite]

From here a detour to Dalegarth Force (formerly known as Stanley Gill Force and still indicated as such on some O. S. maps) should be made. It takes only half an hour and it is well worth a visit, particularly after rain. Turn right up the track, leaving it shortly by a gate on your left, to enter the wooded area of Stanley Gill. A delightful path now leads up alongside the beck. As the ravine narrows, the beck has to be crossed by two wooden footbridges, the last of these being the viewpoint for the falls and the end of the path. Retrace your steps to rejoin the main route.

Ignoring the paths off to your left go through four more gates (there are seven between the barn and the Hall) to pass Dalegarth Hall on your left and, after a stile, a track leading from Dalegarth Hall is reached. Dalegarth Hall is an interesting old farmstead, formerly a large manor house. Note its large round chimneys.

Descend the track to pass a car park in trees on your right, and join the narrow lane which crosses the bridge over the River Esk. This is soon left by a track at an acute angle on your right. Go through a gate and continue to follow the enclosed track until a T-junction is reached with St Catherine's Church on your right. This is the parish church of Eskdale, a plain structure built in the 17th century and more remarkable for the contents of the graveyard than those of the interior. Here is Thomas Dobson's grave, the headstone being inscribed with his own portrait, a fox, a hound and a horn: a work of art in granite. Turn left to walk up the lane and go through a gate. Go straight across at the road running along the valley and proceed up the lane – the main street of Boot – past the inn on your left.

Boot

The village of Boot is the last community of any size in Eskdale, although it is quite small. One feature is the Eskdale corn mill, restored by Cumbria County Council in 1975. A corn mill has been operating in the area since the 13th century and the restored mill has a working water-wheel. There is a permanent exhibition illustrating the techniques of milling grain of different types and there are also displays of Eskdale's farming history. The mill is open to the public from 1 April to 30 September (except Monday) 11.00am–5.00pm and there is an admission charge. The packhorse bridge is more than 250 years old and the path crossing it, which was once a corpse-road, leads to Wasdale Head. Folk were taken from here for burial in Eskdale.

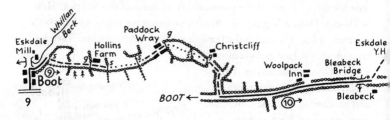

BOOT TO ESKDALE YOUTH HOSTEL

Follow the steep lane out of Boot and ascend to Whillan Beck. Turn right just before the bridge and go over a stile on your right. Follow a fence and then a wall on your right. Continue along the good path above the wall to a gate which leads to Hollins Farm. Pass the farm and, after crossing over a stile, go along the path to follow the wall on your right. Cross a stile and carry on along the track to Paddock Wray farmyard. Pass through the farmyard and through a gate into a field. Then head for a stile leading into another field. Go through a gate and turn right away from the Christcliff farm buildings to follow a track to the narrow road. Turn left at the road and, after passing the Woolpack Inn and going over Bleabeck Bridge, turn left on a track leading to the Eskdale Youth Hostel.

Eskdale Youth Hostel to Coniston Youth Hostel

Distance: 11½ miles (12½ miles including the detour to the summit of Harter Fell)

Going: Moderate to strenuous

Highest point: Walna Scar – 1,990 feet

Map required: O. S. Outdoor Leisure 6 English Lakes, South Western area

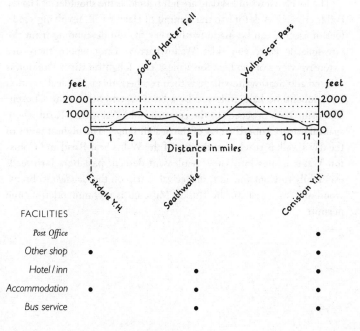

As there are no shops between Eskdale Youth Hostel and Coniston, you may wish to obtain a packed lunch and drinks at the hostel; alternatively there is an inn at Seathwaite. Day Two is a more strenuous walk than Day One but, in good weather, promises magnificent views including what I consider to be the finest view in England – the head of Eskdale and the Scafell range from the slopes leading to the shoulder of Harter Fell. The green valley below makes a striking contrast with the majestic mountains and fells beyond it. The best preserved of the Roman forts in Lakeland can be seen below right across the valley. This is *Mediobognvm*, commonly referred to as Hardknott Castle or Fort, which acted as a defence against an approach from the coast and was built soon after AD 120.

The lovely views of Eskdale are left behind as the shoulder of Harter Fell is crossed. A detour to the summit of Harter Fell, involving 1,000 feet of ascent, can be made by the very fit. On descending from the Grassguards Pass, you skirt Wallowbarrow Crag where there are extensive views of the Duddon Valley. The delightful River Duddon is crossed and Seathwaite village is then reached; this is an ideal location for a lunchtime halt, followed by a brief visit to Seathwaite Church. The route then proceeds to the centuries-old Walna Scar Road where again there are superb views of the Scafell range. The highest point of the day's walk is reached at the top of the Walna Scar Road and Coniston Water comes into view. A pleasant descent past Boo Tarn leads eventually to Coniston and, on arrival, a trip on the *Gondola* to Brantwood and/or a visit to the Ruskin Museum is recommended if time permits.

From the youth hostel, retrace your steps back along the track and go right to pass back over Bleabeck Bridge. After the Woolpack Inn, turn left down a narrow lane which leads to Doctor Bridge across the River Esk. Go through a gate and along the farm road. Pass through two gates in front of Penny Hill farmhouse to an enclosed way and at the end go through a third gate. Continue through a small field to a fourth gate. Soon after entering the large field keep right to ascend the tractor track to go through another gate. After yet another gate, follow the intake wall on your left and ignore the green path to your right. A signpost indicates the direction to Harter Fell. Cross a beck and ascend steeply away from the wall. At the top of this path there are fine views of the head of Eskdale and the Scafell range.

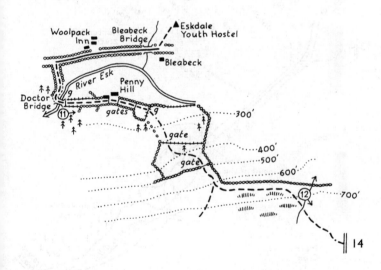

Descend to cross Spothow Gill and ascend from the gill to a stile. Follow the fence on your right and ascend along a reasonable path. Continuing on the main route, go through a gate to enter the woods as the top of the pass is reached. From time to time, due to tree felling and the planting of new trees, changes may occur in this area. Follow the path through the woods in a south-easterly direction and then, at a way-marker, head in a southerly direction and leave by another gate. As you emerge from the woods take the descending path to cross Grassguards Gill; Green Crag and Ulpha Fell are seen on your right. Walk down beside the gill, sometimes rather marshy, until a gate is reached which leads towards the farm of Grassguards. After a second gate ignore a footbridge and ford on your left.

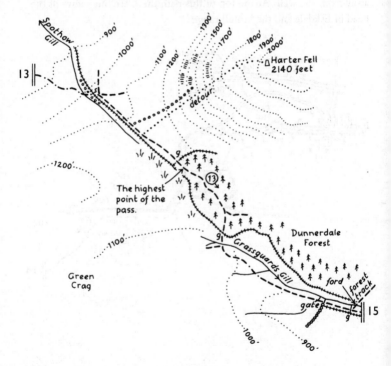

Detour to Harter Fell [*see* map opposite]

Just after a broken wall and prior to a gate and woods, an interesting detour may be made to the top of Harter Fell for those fit enough. With the collapsed wall to your left there is a steep climb amongst heather leading to an exciting summit, the highest part being reached by a simple scramble up naked rock. From the summit, the Scafell group and Upper Eskdale can be seen to the north; Pillar, Red Pike, Scoat Fell and Illgill Head to the north-west; Green Crag to the south-west; the Coniston and Seathwaite Fells to the ESE, and the Fairfield group of mountains, Crinkle Crags and Bowfell to the north-east. However, before embarking on the 1,000 feet of ascent, remember that, later in the day, you have to descend the Duddon Valley and then ascend to the top of the Walna Scar Road.

GRASSGUARDS TO SEATHWAITE

Now pass through the main buildings of Grassguards Farm and, after a gate on the other side of the farm, a track leads between a wall and a fence/hedge. Soon after passing through two more gates, the track undulates between heather and small outcrops. After going through another gate in a wall, Wallowbarrow Crag, owned by the National Trust, is skirted on your left. The path descends to run alongside and then cross Rake Beck before zigzagging steeply through trees. Eventually a gate is reached which leads out of the wood. Another gate is soon reached and a track then descends to go through a third gate and to pass to the left of High Wallowbarrow Farm. Continue to a fourth gate and, after a field, enter the woods through yet another gate.

Follow the path to the footbridge over the River Duddon. The river has its source on the fells above the Wrynose Pass and was a favourite river of Wordsworth who wrote many sonnets in its honour. Turn right and follow the river until it joins Tarn Beck which is crossed by a footbridge. The path ascends through trees to a stile leading onto a road. Turn left and walk into the hamlet of Seathwaite, past the Newfield Inn. [*cont. opposite*]

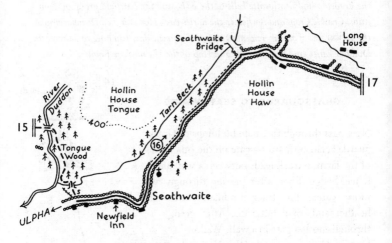

Seathwaite

This hamlet is an ideal lunchtime stop and this may include a visit to the Newfield Inn, although do not drink too much as the Walna Scar Road still has to be climbed to more than 1,900 feet. Seathwaite's Church of the Holy Trinity, built in 1874, replaced an earlier building about which Wordsworth wrote one of his thirty-five Duddon sonnets. In the church is a memorial plaque to Reverend Walker (1709–1802) who was the parson of the old church for sixty-seven years and to whom Wordsworth refers in the sonnet as one 'whose good works form an endless retinue'. Because of his good works, he became known as 'Wonderful Walker'. In the church is one of the chairs he made himself; outside the porch is a stone used by Wonderful Walker to assist with clipping sheep and so inscribed.

From the church, it is about ½ mile to Seathwaite Bridge. Do not cross the bridge. Instead take a track to the right which leads past Hollins House Haw on your right and Long House on your left.

After going through a gate, pass but do not cross a bridge on the Water Board road. Follow the Walna Scar Road for a while, running alongside Long House Gill, and head away from the gill to a gate in a wall. Continue to ascend the Walna Scar Road which gradually becomes better graded, swinging left shortly after the wall. From here, on a clear day, there are fine views of the Scafell range of mountains towards the north-west. A tiny cairn marks the highest point of the road. This was once an important route across the hills, linking the Duddon Valley with Coniston. The rough track still services a slate quarry high on the slopes of Old Man, but the horses that laboured here have been replaced by walkers who are rewarded with excellent views of the Coniston Fells. Between the upper valley of the River Duddon and Coniston village are distinct summits rising to above 2,500 feet.

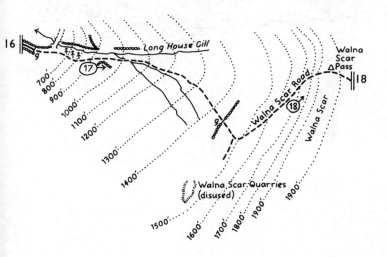

From the moorland-type setting, descend through rock outcrops and cairns, zigzagging steeply. After a squelchy section Cove Bridge is reached: this is not named on the Ordnance Survey map but was named by Wainwright in his Pictorial Guide. Shortly afterwards, a large cairn is reached on your right. This signals the departure of a path up to Goat's Water and onto the ridge between Dow Crag and Coniston Old Man. The main path descends in earnest to pass between two small rock gateways. It levels off to lead on an unmistakable track to Boo Tarn. Bronze Age antiquities have been found at Boo Tarn and in 1954 a boy photographed a flying saucer there.

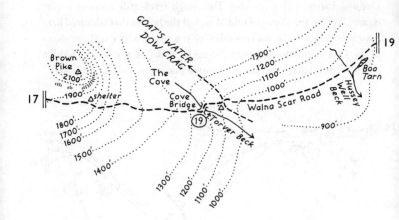

From Boo Tarn descend gently across the open fell until the track meets a gate. Continue straight on along the road, now tarmac, until it starts to descend steeply beside a small beck, eventually leading to the centre of Coniston. Turn left after the Sun Hotel and take the A593 Ambleside road into the centre of the village. Depending on what time you reach Coniston you will have an opportunity to visit some of the shops, perhaps to purchase a postcard to send home to report 2 days completed, 12 to go. From the village, turn left down a road between the Black Bull and the Co-op and follow it beside Church Beck, passing the Ruskin Museum on your right. Take a path on the right towards Far End and soon turn right, at a gate, which then leads to the youth hostel on your right.

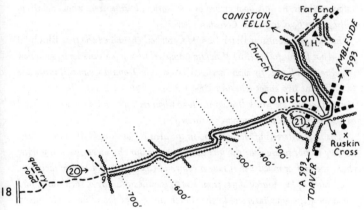

Coniston

The best-known resident of Coniston was the Victorian writer John Ruskin who lived at Brantwood on the east side of the lake from 1871 to 1900. The house, now administered by an educational trust, is open to the public from mid March to mid November, daily, and during the winter from Wednesdays to Sundays. An admission charge is payable. Brantwood contains many items associated with Ruskin including paintings by his protégé, William Turner. Ruskin's ideas on education inspired people in many countries and there is a Ruskin Museum in the village where one of the main exhibits is a linen pall worked with Ruskin lace, made by women of the area to cover his body for his burial in Coniston churchyard (which he preferred to Westminster Abbey). Ruskin no doubt sailed up and down the Coniston Water aboard the steam ship Gondola which still carries tourists and walkers across the lake, calling at Brantwood. The boat was launched in 1859 and can carry eighty-six passengers in her comfortable saloons. She is the only boat owned by the National Trust, from whom details of sailings can be obtained at Coniston pier.

In 1939 on Coniston Water Donald Campbell christened the first Bluebird powerboat for his father (Sir) Malcolm Campbell who, a few days later, set a new world record of 141.74 mph. Between 1956—59, Donald Campbell broke the world record five times (the last time reaching 276.33 mph). On 4 January 1967, however, he was killed on the lake when trying to raise the world record to 300 mph. His body was never recovered.

The most interesting old building in the area is Coniston Hall, a late 16th-century manor house near the lake shore. Its circular chimneys give it a unique character and grandeur; it is now a centre of camp sites and leisure facilities. The church of St. Andrew dates from 1819, is built naturally of local slate, and has a most spacious interior. In the churchyard can be found an Anglo-Saxon type of cross commemorating John Ruskin.

Coniston Youth Hostel to Windermere Youth Hostel

Distance: 12½ miles (13 miles including the detour to Town End)

Going: Moderate

Highest point: Hundreds Road – 820 feet

Map required: O.S. Outdoor Leisure 7 English Lakes, South
 Western area

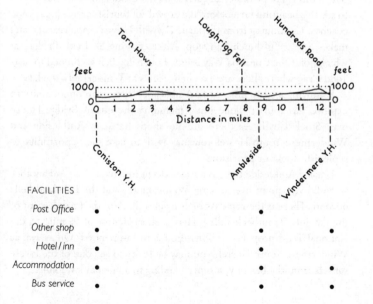

FACILITIES			
Post Office	●	●	
Other shop	●	●	●
Hotel / inn	●	●	
Accommodation	●	●	●
Bus service	●	●	●

There are three moderate climbs and descents on this third day but the resulting sweeping views across the Lakeland Fells make the effort well worthwhile. When originally planning this day's walk, I had intended to take the ferry across Windermere the lake. However the long-distance walkers' 'ethics' committee (an ad hoc group that usually meets in a public house) decided that this would not be in the true spirit of a coast to coast *walk*. The only alternative was to head north or south around Windermere, England's largest lake. The northern route proved more attractive and results in a superb day's walking.

The route follows the Cumbria Way from Coniston to Skelwith Bridge. After retrospective views of Coniston Water, Tarn Hows is reached where a short break can be taken to admire what is now a famous tourist attraction. It is best viewed outside the tourist season but, if this is not possible, an early start from Coniston will enable you to see this beautiful tarn before the crowds of tourists arrive in cars and coaches. Continuing from the tarn, Colwith Force is soon reached and makes a peaceful lunchtime stop. After crossing Skelwith Bridge, at which point the Cumbria Way is left, Loughrigg Fell is climbed to near Todd Crag where there are excellent views of Windermere the lake.

Following a steep descent to Ambleside, there is an opportunity to explore this tourist 'honeypot', including the quaint Bridge House over Stock Ghyll. As there are no shops between Ambleside and Windermere Youth Hostel you may wish to take the opportunity to replenish stocks or provisions.

Leaving Ambleside there is a steep ascent to Jenkin Crag, yet another splendid viewpoint overlooking Windermere, and the Lakeland Fells beyond. There is then an easy high-level walk until the final descent of the day into Troutbeck valley. Here a short detour of ½ mile to the National Trust property of Town End is recommended. On arrival at Windermere Youth Hostel, you may be lucky to see one of the lovely sunsets from the balcony; a superb ending to a fine day's walking.

Leave the youth hostel and turn right into a lane. Keep straight on until the A593 is reached. Cross this road and shortly Yewdale Beck will be on your left. At Shepherd Bridge turn left to cross the bridge. Go over a stile on your left and turn right to leave the beck to ascend the path to a gate by a ruined byre with an ornate 'castle' front. Follow the wire fence to pass through a gate in a wall; an excellent retrospective view of Coniston Water can be seen from here. Follow the path ahead, crossing a stile to enter a small wood (owned by the National Trust). Leave the wood by another stile and continue forward for 300 yards before veering left through a gateway. Cross the field ahead to a gate and then follow the track left to Low Yewdale, commonly referred to as Yewdale Farm. Close to the farm and before crossing a stone bridge, go over a stile on your right and cross the field, following parallel to the beck to reach the next stile; this leads into Tarn Hows Wood (also owned by the National Trust). Follow the path ahead which shortly

bears right and uphill through the woods. It is easy to follow, going over a wooden bridge and passing a stile leading into an enclosed fenced area; do not go over the stile. A second wooden bridge is crossed and a second stile leading out of the enclosure is passed.

Shortly after a wall is joined on your left Tarn Hows Cottage comes into view. Pass through two gates to enter a farmyard and turn right through a gate to a track leading, at another gate, to the Tarn Hows road which is followed to the left. After a car park in woods on your right turn left off the road to see the romantic Tarn Hows.

TARN HOWS TO SKELWITH BRIDGE

Pass round the left-hand side of the tarn (there is also a track around to the right) and where the two paths join at a signposted Y-junction take the path (signed for Arnside and Langdales) bending slightly left, then continue in a northerly direction. The path is followed to a gate and a ladder-stile onto a rough road. Turn left down the track.

Tarn Hows

This is one of the great honeypots of British tourism, with an estimated 750,000 visitors a year. This most perfect of Lakeland landscapes is man-made. Until the last century there was a collection of small pools here known as Monk Coniston Tarns or The Tarns, and it wasn't until a small dam was built across the outflow stream, Tom Gill, that this famous spectacle of water was created. The Ordnance Survey still call it 'The Tarns' on their maps.

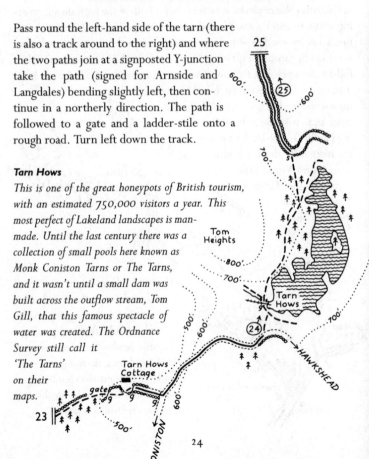

Continue on this track until it reaches the Coniston–Ambleside road, A593. Cross the road to a track and then immediately go right to follow a permissive path which leads to a stile. After crossing the stile, continue along this path which runs inside the wall and protects the walker from the traffic. Return to the road by a ladder-stile, and almost immediately two metalled roads lead off to the left. Take the second road, signposted High Park, and continue to High Park Farm. Enter the farm through a gate on your right and, after leaving the farm by another gate, follow the way-marked route to a wood. Enter the wood (owned by the National Trust) and take the permissive path to the left which descends to Colwith Force. The falls' peaceful setting amongst woodland makes it an appropriate place to rest awhile and perhaps have some refreshments. Here the River Brathay is enclosed and twists between rocks and woods on its journey between Little Langdale Tarn and Elterwater. Follow the path which leads to a stile and the road near a bridge. Across the road to the right of the bridge, there is a stile in the wall which you cross into a small field and take a steep, well-defined path through the woods.

Colwith Force
(waterfall)

ELTERWATER

River Brathay

400'

High Park
Farm

9

400'

TARN HOWS

27

26

26

A 593 AMBLESIDE

stile

500'

600' 500'

A 593 CONISTON

24

Leave the woods at a gate and continue along the path to cross three stiles and pass Low Park Farm. Continue along the clear path to pass through Park Farm and shortly turn right, following the wall on your right, to go through a gate. At a building go through two more gates to follow the track until it bears right, at which point you continue ahead on a path. Go through two gates to join the Coniston–Ambleside road just before Skelwith Bridge. Turn left down the main road towards the bridge.

SKELWITH BRIDGE TO AMBLESIDE

Cross the bridge and where the main road bears right, just before the telephone booth, take the lane ahead leading to Little Loughrigg. Continue to climb the steep lane until a T-junction is reached. Turn right for a short distance, then turn left off the lane onto a drive which leads up towards Tarn Foot camping site and some cottages. Turn right and from here the route is signed to Ambleside. Pass the cottages and then, at a junction, continue ahead through a gate.

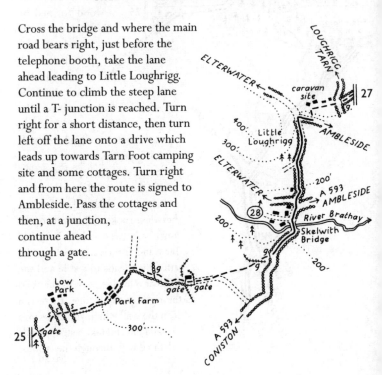

The path follows an enclosed way to a gate and then runs along the foot of Loughrigg Fell, following a sturdy stone wall. Approximately 300 yards after leaving the wall, at a path junction, turn 90 degrees SSE and cross a beck to pick up a path bearing slightly right by the wall bend. The path continues with a wall on your right and this is your guide. After a gate in a fence, the path goes through a wall gap and begins to veer away from the wall. Ignoring paths off to your right and left it then skirts a couple of small tarns and passes close to a much larger tarn, Lily Tarn. Just past the end of this turn left.

Detour to the viewpoint
For a superb view of Windermere don't turn left at Lily Tarn, but go straight on to a complex junction of paths and ascend the crags ahead. From the summit, the outline of Galava, a Roman fort, can be seen near the northern tip of Windermere the lake. Retrace your steps to Lily Tarn.

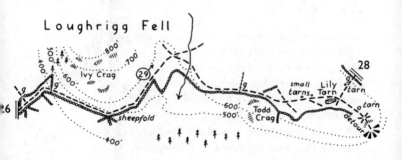

On the main route from Lily Tarn pass to the right of a small tarn or wet patch visible ahead. After passing this, descend to go through a kissing gate.

Descend towards a gap between woods and squeeze through a stile to follow an enclosed way and then bear right down steps to a lane in front of Brow Head Farm. Turn right through a gate and descend the lane to, after another gate, a minor road. Go very slightly right and then left over Miller Bridge. Take the right-hand path through Rothay Park which eventually enters a lane leading past the school on your left and the church on your right.

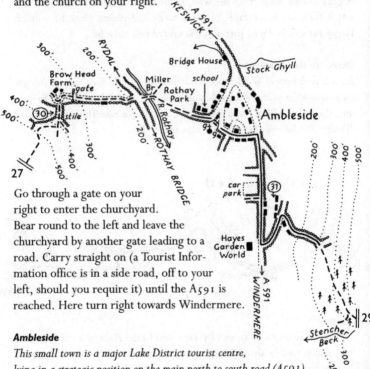

Go through a gate on your right to enter the churchyard. Bear round to the left and leave the churchyard by another gate leading to a road. Carry straight on (a Tourist Information office is in a side road, off to your left, should you require it) until the A591 is reached. Here turn right towards Windermere.

Ambleside

This small town is a major Lake District tourist centre, lying in a strategic position on the main north to south road (A591). It is a place for coast to coasters to replenish stocks and experience the second Lake District 'honeypot' of the day.

The Romans showed their appreciation of Ambleside's strategic attractions in AD79 when they built Galava. The site of the fort has been excavated and

Roman artefacts can be seen at a permanent 'Man in Lakeland' exhibition near Waterhead. This is designed to help visitors discover and appreciate the Lake District's distinctive heritage.

For those spending a while in the town, Ambleside has many remnants of the 17th century, including the tiny Bridge House perched over Stock Ghyll; it was built as a summer house for the former Ambleside Hall. It once housed a family of six and is now owned by the National Trust and is their oldest information centre and their smallest shop.

AMBLESIDE TO WINDERMERE YOUTH HOSTEL

Follow the A591 south until opposite Hayes Garden World on your right. Take the minor road that joins on your left at an acute angle, then soon turn right along a surfaced lane. At a fork keep right along a level track which then starts to ascend to enter woods. This is the National Trust-owned Skelghyll Wood.

The track starts to ascend until Jenkin Crag viewpoint is soon reached; this offers fine views across Windermere the lake and in the distance much of the route followed earlier in the day. Leave the woods by a gate and carry on to another gate leading to High Skelghyll Farm which, via two more gates, is passed. Join a lane and follow it for a short distance to a bridge and then go through a gate immediately on your left. Continue along the path, first ascending, and then descending to a ford. Cross this and ascend through two gates.

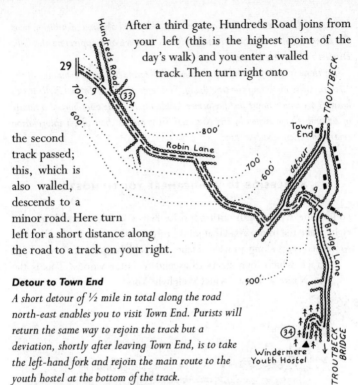

After a third gate, Hundreds Road joins from your left (this is the highest point of the day's walk) and you enter a walled track. Then turn right onto

the second track passed; this, which is also walled, descends to a minor road. Here turn left for a short distance along the road to a track on your right.

Detour to Town End

A short detour of ½ mile in total along the road north-east enables you to visit Town End. Purists will return the same way to rejoin the track but a deviation, shortly after leaving Town End, is to take the left-hand fork and rejoin the main route to the youth hostel at the bottom of the track.

This house was built in 1626 by George Browne, and was occupied by the Browne family until 1944. One of the finest examples of a yeoman farmer's house in the Lake District, it was acquired by the National Trust in 1947. It is open from 1–5pm 1 April to 30 October, daily excluding Saturdays and Mondays, except Bank Holiday Mondays.

If not visiting Town End descend the track through two gates to another minor road, Bridge Lane. If staying at the youth hostel (named High Cross Castle on the Ordnance Survey map), turn right onto the lane and walk for ½ mile along the lane until the hostel is reached by turning up the second lane on the right into a wooded area.

Windermere Youth Hostel to Burneside

Distance: 12 miles (12 ½ miles including the deviation to Staveley)

Going: Easy

Highest point: Orrest Head – 781 feet

Map required: O. S. Outdoor Leisure 7 English Lakes, South
Eastern area

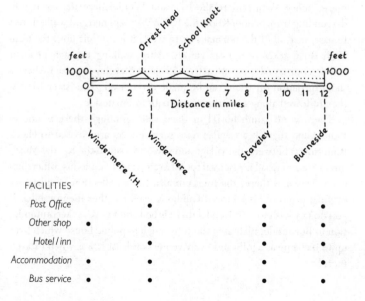

FACILITIES	Windermere Y.H.	Windermere	Staveley	Burneside
Post Office		●	●	●
Other shop	●	●	●	●
Hotel / inn		●	●	●
Accommodation	●	●	●	●
Bus service	●	●	●	●

On this fourth day there is an opportunity to give aching muscles a rest since the route passes over easier terrain, and the distance is relatively short. The walk leaves the pleasant green valley of Troutbeck, surrounded by the imposing peaks of Yoke, Ill Bell and Froswick, and soon reaches one of the highlights of the entire walk, Orrest Head. Apart from admiring the panoramic views of Windermere the lake, this is a place to remember Alfred Wainwright who came here on his first holiday to the Lake District and began his 'love affair' with the area. Like Haystacks it is a place of pilgrimage for Wainwright admirers.

A pleasant descent through woods leads to Windermere the town where there are plenty of opportunities to replenish stocks. Leaving Windermere, there is the ascent of School Knott where there are good views back towards Windermere the lake, and Windermere the town. Wainwright often reminds us in his books that it is *never* Lake Windermere, hence Windermere the lake and Windermere the town. On descending from School Knott the Dales Way is joined and walked west to east, instead of the normal east to west; it is not left until the Cam High Road takes over near Hawes. After walking through pleasant rolling countryside, the attractive village of Staveley is passed where a short deviation off-route can be made if required. The River Kent is then followed along a clear, pleasant path to Burneside.

There is no youth hostel in Burneside, although there is one in Kendal and there is a regular train service (you are advised to check train times) between the village and town. A visit to the Kendal Museum in Station Road is essential for all Wainwright fans as his 'office' has been recreated there: the museum also has a collection of thirty-six original pages of his Pictorial Guides as well as other memorabilia. If you do not wish to visit Kendal there is bed and breakfast accommodation in Burneside, including the Jolly Anglers public house which lives up to its name as a jolly and lively venue – at least it was when I stayed there!

From the youth hostel re-trace the route north along the lane for ½ mile and take the track on your right which descends between walls to cross two footbridges over Trout Beck. After a gate ascend the track and go through another gate to join the A592. Turn right and, not long after a road forks off to the left, take a grassy terraced path on your left. Go through a gate just before two cottages and then, after a second gate, cross a minor road to follow a tarmac road. At a drive leading to a farmyard bear left along another drive to a gate, and then at a barn at Far Orrest go through a gate ahead and then immediately turn left (ignore the footpath sign that incorrectly points ahead to the cottage) over a ladder-stile and cut across a small field. Go through two gates to cross an attractive walled path, and then turn right to follow the wall on your right to another gate. Use this to cross a farm track and go through a fifth gate. Head across a field to go over a stile and

then go slightly left to cross another stile. Follow the wall on your left to the next stile. After the stile, the path has been redirected to go through two gates, keeping right to circumnavigate the farm buildings at Near Orrest.

34

After a stile, turn right at the minor road and follow it for a short way to then go over another stile on your left. Follow the path along a wall and then head south, ignoring paths left and right, to go over a stile and ascend on a grassy path to the Orrest Head viewpoint.

From the viewpoint, descend to pass through an iron gate to a track going right beside a wall in pleasant woodland. Ignore paths off to your left until, after a 'dog-leg' left and right, the track descends with a wall on your right. At a T-junction keep left and soon a lane is joined. At the main road turn left and after 100 yards, taking care of passing traffic, cross the road towards the entrance to the station where you gain the safety of a pavement.

WINDERMERE TO STAVELEY

Continue to ascend the main A591 in the direction of Kendal. Orrest Head Farm is passed on the right after 350 yards, and 200 yards further on Alice Howe Farm is also passed on your right. Continue uphill for a further 200 yards to locate and go through a wooden gate on your right which leads into rough pasture land.

From the gate, follow the cart track to reach a fork. Bear right to pass through a wooden gate. Continue along the track and in the opposite corner of this field (just before a gate) turn left over a ladder-stile. [cont. opposite]

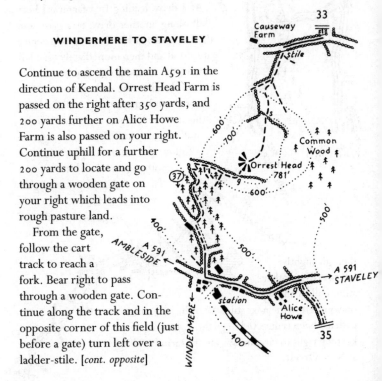

34

Then follow the wall on your right which soon bends sharply to the right and becomes a wire fence; follow this to a stile. Being vigilant of passing trains, cross the railway line to enter the field opposite by a second stile. Follow the well-defined footpath and shortly turn left to climb over a ladder-stile. Cross over a beck and turn right onto a hard-surfaced track. Shortly take a left fork and further on reach a gate across the route. On the other side of the gate turn left and follow a grassy path which ascends in varying grades of steepness alongside the left-hand wall to reach a gate. Having gone through the gate bear left and almost immediately right and looking ahead you will see that School Knott resembles the shape of a saddle. Follow the path uphill (indistinct at times) to aim for the highest peak which is seen slightly left of centre. To leave the top, locate School Knott Tarn which can be seen 350 yards away on the other side of this hill to the south-east. Descend across the grass directly towards the tarn, and pass through a walker's gate adjacent to a field gate. Walk towards the edge of this secluded tarn, then bear right to walk alongside a gully. After 200 yards, take the kissing gate on your left. Here the route joins the Dales Way and marches with it for the next 40 miles until the Cam High Road near Hawes is reached. Ascend half-left to the junction of collapsed walls. The path skirts marshy land to a wall gap and then descends to a stile in a facing wall. Follow another ruinous wall on your left and after going through it pass through a gate to the yard at Hag End, and walk between the buildings.

34

38

stiles

Gill Cottage

500'

600'

700'

School Knott
760'

gate

gate

School Knott
Tarn

39

gate

700'

Hag
End

stile

36

700'

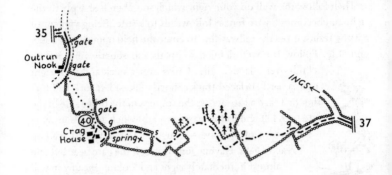

Take the access track leading to the lane and then turn right. After going through a gate, the farm buildings at Outrun Nook are shortly reached. Turn left through a kissing-gate, pass round some trees in the centre of the field and ascend to a facing gate in the far corner. As the next farm, Crag House, is approached, turn left along the track until the front of a large modern barn is reached. Keeping near to the wall on your left, go through a gate and descend towards a stile. Just before the stile there is a spring which goes underground after a couple of yards. The shortest stream after the longest lake. Go over the stile and then skirt some gorse bushes to ascend to a gate. After the gate, continue along a track which then bears right to skirt a small fenced plantation. Bear left to go through a gate and follow a sketchy path which crosses the field, gradually drawing closer to the wall on your right until a gate is reached. This leads to a green bridleway between walls which shortly reaches a lane; turn right onto this.

The lane descends to the farm of Fell Plain, after which turn left into another lane. This climbs to the brow of a hill before descending through two gates to New Hall Farm (at the second gate the right of way goes off to the right but common usage is to continue ahead), opposite which take a track to the left. Go through a gate and then descend along the outside of a wood. Go through a kissing-gate and down a field to another gate. At the bottom turn right into a narrow surfaced drive, Field Close.

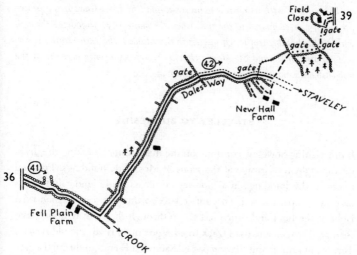

Field Close leads to a lane. Turn left and the lane will pass over the busy A591 which now bypasses Staveley.

Deviation to Staveley

A decision now needs to be made whether to make a short deviation off route to Staveley, by continuing along this lane, past the station and then returning by the old main road to Sandyhill Farm. The deviation adds just over ½ mile to the route but gives an opportunity to obtain provisions and refreshments.

This village, with its narrow main street and tiny River Gowan, is a peaceful haven now compared to the time when the main A591 thundered through with all the holiday traffic. Of interest in the village is the 14th-century tower, sole survivor of the old St. Mary's church. Staveley was once a centre of the wood-turning industry, particularly bobbin making.

STAVELEY TO BURNESIDE

If not visiting Staveley, continue on the main route by taking the drive on the right to a garage at the front of Moss Side buildings. Proceed between the buildings in a 'dog-leg' to cross a stile and, after Moss Side, accompany a wall on your left to go through a gate, then turn right at the field end. Turn left to go through the railway underpass, then go down an enclosed track to emerge onto a road (the old A591). Turn right onto it and, having passed Sandyhill Farm, go through a gate on your left to follow an enclosed path. The Ordnance Survey map may no longer be correct at this point in that the Dales Way has been re-routed; new editions will no doubt include this revision. Go through a gate and bear left to go through another one. Immediately turn right and after going through a gate follow the wall on the left which runs between you and the River Kent. Go through another gate and follow the path next to the river. Go over a stile near woods.

This path leads to a narrow rocky section and then another gate. Follow the river to a stile; here the Lake District National Park is left. Do not be too disappointed, there is the Yorkshire Dales National Park

[*cont. opposite*]

to look forward to on the following day. Go through a wall gap and, after rugged woodland, go over a stile to pass a barn at two gates

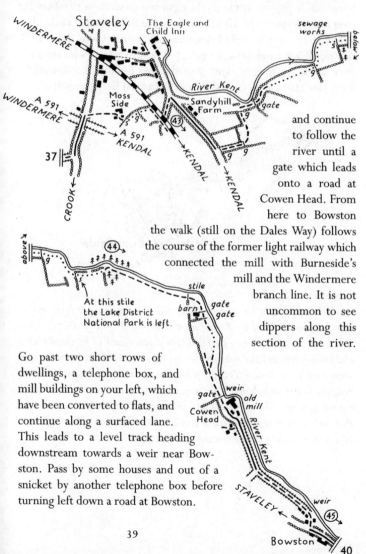

and continue to follow the river until a gate which leads onto a road at Cowen Head. From here to Bowston the walk (still on the Dales Way) follows the course of the former light railway which connected the mill with Burneside's mill and the Windermere branch line. It is not uncommon to see dippers along this section of the river.

Go past two short rows of dwellings, a telephone box, and mill buildings on your left, which have been converted to flats, and continue along a surfaced lane. This leads to a level track heading downstream towards a weir near Bowston. Pass by some houses and out of a snicket by another telephone box before turning left down a road at Bowston.

Follow the Burneside road (pronounced Burneyside) for a short distance and then take the lane on your left and cross Bowston Bridge. Immediately go over a stile on the right and down steps to follow the river now on your right. Head away from the river towards a stile; then follow a fence on your right to another stile. Turn left away from a mill-race on the river and through a gate; follow the fence on your right and after another gate turn right onto the lane leading into Burneside. Burneside Hall can be viewed to your left as you face the road.

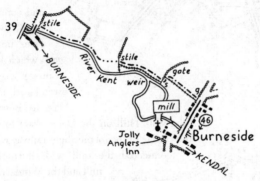

Burneside

This village is famous for its paper mills and one in particular dominates it. There have been mills on the River Kent at Burneside at least since 1283, when there is known to have been a corn mill. The parish church of St. Oswald has a solid tower of typical Lakeland construction. Burneside Hall dates from the 14th century and is an excellent example of a hall-house with a pele tower incorporated into it. Strictly a defensive measure, it afforded shelter from border raids by marauding Scots. Generally the raiders, or reivers as they were known, were more interested in cattle rustling than in battles. The Hall is now a farmhouse and there is an impressive gatehouse across the courtyard.

Burnside to Sedbergh

Distance: 16 miles (16½ miles including the detour to the Brigflatts
Meeting House)

Going: Easy – moderate

Highest point: Old Scotch Road (shortly after the M6) – 725 feet

Map required: O.S. Outdoor Leisure 7 English Lakes, South Eastern
area and O.S. Outdoor Leisure 19 Howgill Fells and Upper Eden Valley

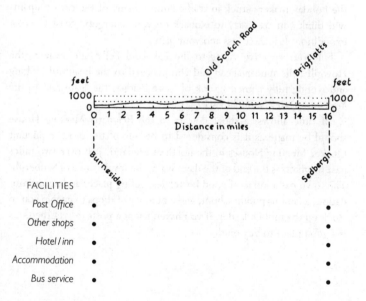

Although the terrain is less hilly than the previous four days, there is an increase in the mileage covered and some time-consuming route-finding through many farms, gates and stiles. It is suggested that an early start is made and that adequate provisions are carried for the day as there are few opportunities to obtain them *en route*. However, the countryside is pleasant throughout with undulating hills, panoramic views and fine riverside walking. The Dales Way is followed for the entire day but note that most Dales Way signposts are pointing in the opposite direction. After leaving the River Kent at Burneside, the rivers Sprint, Mint, Lune and Rawthey are all encountered. The middle part of the day's walk involves a brief unwelcome reminder of 'modern life' as a bridge takes you over the noisy, snaking M6 and leads to the highest point of the day, the now quiet Old Scotch Road – formerly the main road to Scotland! Do not feel guilty if you reflect on all the holiday-makers stuck in traffic jams – many of the car occupants will think you are crazy to embark on your energetic coast to coast expedition. It is their loss and your gain.

Fine retrospective views to the Lakeland Fells fade away as the Howgill Fells appear ahead and you proceed to the beautiful looking and wonderfully named Crook of Lune Bridge, the 'gateway' to the Yorkshire Dales National Park.

If time allows, a short detour to the Brigflatts Meeting House should be made as it is considered to be one of the most important Quaker Meeting Houses in the north of England. Just over two miles past Brigflatts is the end of the day's walk, the lovely town of Sedbergh. The town has a range of good hostelries, eating places and accommodation, a famous public school, and a number of shops to enable you to stock up the mobile larder. If you haven't sent a postcard yet then this is a good place to buy one!

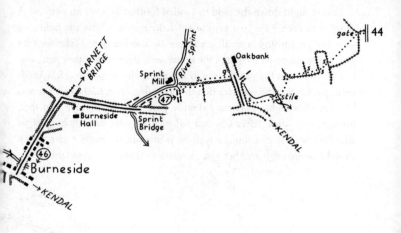

BURNESIDE TO BLACK MOSS TARN

Retrace your steps from the day before along the lane which leads out of the village; Burneside Hall can be seen on your right. At the T-junction turn right along the road until Sprint Bridge is crossed. Take the stile on your left immediately after the bridge and follow the River Sprint on your left. On the other side of the river is Sprint Mill which is an example of a water-powered textile mill of the late 18th century. Cross a stile and follow the wall on your left. Cross another stile to continue on the other side of the wall. Go through a gate and at Oakbank turn right along the lane. At the road junction go over a stile on your left to join a path which leads to a bridge over the steam. Cross this and a stile and then head half-left to a short wall section in the bottom corner of the field which is crossed by a stile. Go over an intervening stile and over a modest brow and descend to another two stiles. Then keep left away from the corner of the field rising towards a gate. Go through the gate.

Pass straight down the field to a stiled footbridge over an outflow. A short path then runs to a prominent ladder-stile. Cross the field to a gate and go through a small enclosure to another gate. Take another gate to the immediate right of the house and, after yet another gate, follow the drive to the gated A6. Go left along the verge for a few yards then, paying the utmost attention to the traffic, cross to the quiet access lane on your right. This rises steeply past Tarn Bank Farm and then through two gates. After Garnett Folds and a gate, initially keep right and then head away from the wall on your right to another gate. Keep straight on through another gate. Continue along an access lane.

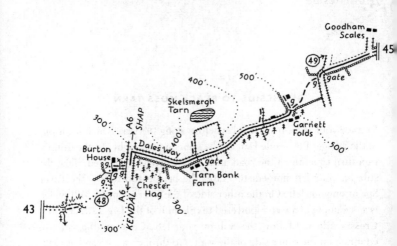

The lane soon leads to a largely enclosed path and a gate. Continue ahead to a gate near the farm of New House. Pass to the right of the house, then through the yard and another gate. Ascend the field beyond towards an obtrusive pylon and then descend to the northern bank of Black Moss Tarn.

BLACK MOSS TARN TO GREEN HEAD FARM

Follow the fence away from the tarn to cross a stile. Keep left to cross another stile and head across the field to yet another stile. With the fence on your right, cross a narrow pasture and where the field narrows, head past a collapsed wall to yet another stile. Follow the enclosed way to go over a stile and through a gate, and pass in front of the house at Biglands. At this point the 50-mile marker is reached, a time to celebrate with a quarter of the total distance covered. Keep right to go along the drive to reach a lane which is crossed to a narrow enclosed way, shortly leading to a gate.

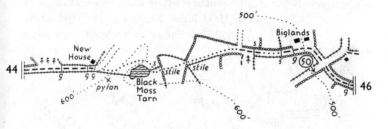

Enter the yard of a house and, after leaving it by a gate, bear right to another gate and follow the path which runs parallel with a track on the left before joining the track at an iron kissing-gate. Follow this enclosed green lane to a second iron kissing-gate on your left. Descend the field to a footbridge over the River Mint, at this point a small and meandering tributary of the River Kent which it joins at Kendal. Then bear right, rising to a gate in the facing hedge. Join another path leading away from a barn on your left and, on reaching a hedge, turn left to follow it to a stile just over the brow. A short descent leads to a hurdle-stile in the facing hedge. After this stile continue descending to a gate which leads to the farm road from Thursgill which is followed right (the right of way leaves the track off to the right but common usage is to keep on the track).

Continue ahead to a gate leading to the main road (A685). Cross carefully and then walk right for a short distance before taking the drive on your left which leads to a gate at Grayrigg Foot Farm. Pass between farm buildings to another gate. Follow the wall on your right to a footbridge over the beck. Go through another gate and then follow a faint green path. Before a cattle-grid bear left up an access road to a gate at Green Head Farm. Keeping to the right of the buildings, follow an enclosed track which swings right to another gate.

At long last there is a reasonable stretch of walking without stiles and gates every few yards! The tractor track bears left and then right to lead to a stile which gives access to the main railway line; cross carefully, and cross another stile. Follow the path left to a gate and turn right onto a narrow road opposite a lone building. At the junction at Thatchmoor Head double back to the left and follow the narrow lane. Shortly after some buildings at Hardrigg, cross a stile on your right. Go through a gate and follow the fence on your right. Go through another gate and then through the trees on a clear path which crosses the drive leading to Morsedale Hall. Bear right down the slope to cross a bridge over the beck. Ascend the now enclosed path, past further buildings to a gate. This leads to a stile and then follows a fence on the right down a gentle brow to another stile.

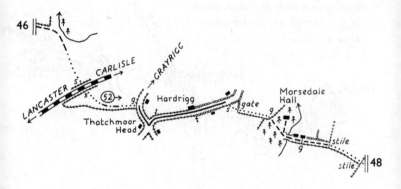

Next head for a stile in a facing wall. Go through two gates and then over a second stile which is on your left. This leads onto a green track. After a third stile pass the buildings on your right at Holme Park. Go through a gate and through a grove to a fourth stile. Go slightly left to a fifth stile and then through a gate onto a lane. Turn left and pass between the farm buildings at Lambrigg Head to go over the stile on your right, leading to a bridge over the roaring M6. Go through a gate on the bridge and keep left aiming for a gap in the wall ahead; follow the wall on your left. Turn left along the quiet 'Old Scotch Road', the highest point of the day's walking. From here there are good views to the Howgill Fells in the ENE, the Lake District in the WNW, Whinfell Beacon to the north and the Lune valley to the NNE. The M6 motorway and main west coast railway line can be seen threading their way north. Shortly cross a stile on your right. Follow a track and then a wall and skirt around Lakethwaite Farm which is on your right. Cross a broken fence which joins a drive leading away from the farm. Shortly go through a gate on your right to follow a track.

Walk past some trees and go over a stile. Follow the line of trees and an enclosed way for just under ½ mile to a stile, which leads to a road at Lowgill. Turn right, right again and then left down a steep narrow lane under the Lowgill Viaduct with its eleven stone arches; this used to serve the now disused Ingleton to Tebay branch line. Continue to descend the steep lane to the Crook of Lune Bridge, the riverbank immediately before the bridge being a lovely spot to stop for a rest and perhaps something to eat. Cross this beautiful, narrow, high-arched bridge. Looking north-east the River Lune, lined on both sides with trees, draws your eyes to the Howgill Fells. As you cross the bridge you enter the Yorkshire Dales National Park; there is no finer 'gateway' to the National Park than this bridge.

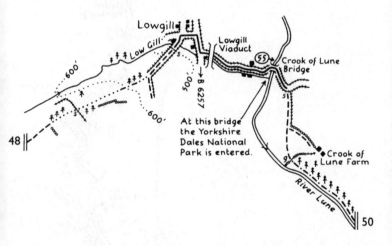

CROOK OF LUNE BRIDGE TO LINCOLN'S INN BRIDGE

From the bridge follow the lane a short distance to a stile on your right. Go over the stile and follow the track (ignoring the track off to your left to the Crook of Lune Farm) to go through a gate. The path enters a pleasant wooded area alongside the river.

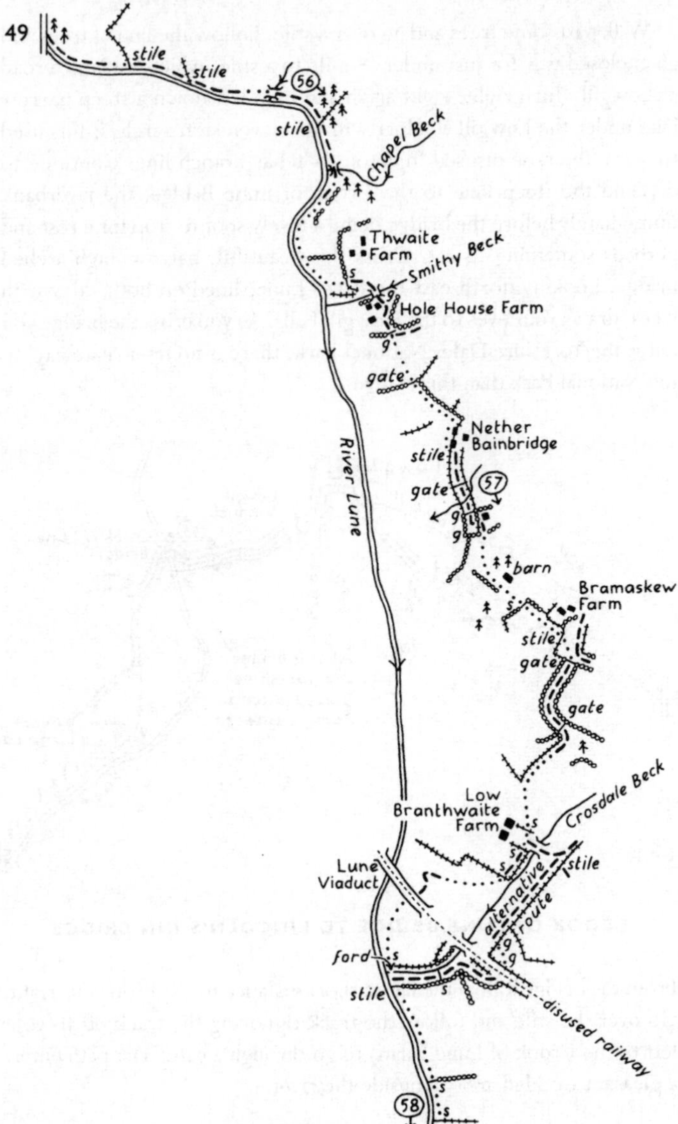

stile   stile

56

stile

Chapel Beck

Thwaite
Farm

Smithy Beck

s

Hole House Farm

g

gate

River Lune

Nether
Bainbridge

stile

gate

57

g
g

barn

Bramaskew
Farm

s

stile

gate

gate

Low
Branthwaite
Farm

s

Crosdale Beck

s

Lune
Viaduct

stile

alternative route

s

ford   s

stile   s

disused railway

s

s

58

Follow the river, crossing over two stiles, a stream, another stile and then a footbridge over Chapel Beck. A ccompany the Lune through a large pasture below Thwaite Farm, then head away from the river to a stile and follow the path to cross over Smithy Beck footbridge. Go through a small gate to pass along the path to the houses ahead. Fork left towards the barns and then go right past them in the yard of Hole House Farm. Go through the gate and ascend to a little brow and then descend to another gate. Follow the wall on your left and then bear right past a barn at Nether Bainbridge to cross a stile on your left. Follow the enclosed track to go through three gates. After going through the gates ascend the large field, past a barn on your left, to a stile. Head past Bramaskew Farm to another stile, and then to a gate leading to an enclosed track. Go through another gate and bear right to descend down a field beside the fence. Turn left at the fence corner to a stile.

As you reach Low Branthwaite Farm a decision needs to be made as to which route to follow. If there has been heavy rain recently, the ford beyond the viaduct ahead may be impassable: *see* below for the alternative route. The main walk follows the 'fair-weather route': cross from stile to stile over Low Branthwaite's access track. Follow a track alongside the fence to another stile. The path swings right and crosses a level pasture before dropping left to descend beneath the arches of Lune Viaduct. Now follow the bank of the River Lune to go over two stiles, the first of which leads to a ford which you cross.

Alternative wet-weather route

After the stile at Low Branthwaite Farm, turn left along an access track and, after crossing Crosdale Beck, immediately turn right to follow the fence to a gate on your left. Then go through a gate to an archway under the dismantled railway line and bear right and then left to go over a stile. Descend to another stile on your left to rejoin the route. You might have the satisfaction of seeing other walkers who braved the main route get a bootful!

Continue along the bank of the River Lune to cross two more stiles and, after two gates, you will reach Lincoln's Inn Bridge.

The bridge is named after an inn that used to be on the opposite bank; it is now a farm. Take care crossing the A684 Kendal to Sedbergh road and go over the stile opposite. The walk now starts to leave the River Lune and gradually bends round to the River Rawthey. The Lune continues on its way to Lancaster, having been born 1,700 feet up in the Howgill Fells. Leaving the bridge, follow the river to a stile and then head away from the river to another stile in the fence. After crossing the stile, curve right and then shortly head left to a gate which leads to an access track. Keep right and then left past Luneside Farm to go through a gate. Follow the enclosed wide track to go through a gate. Continue along the track to a second gate and then follow the winding path to a third gate. After this, follow the pleasant hedged track to High

[cont. opposite]

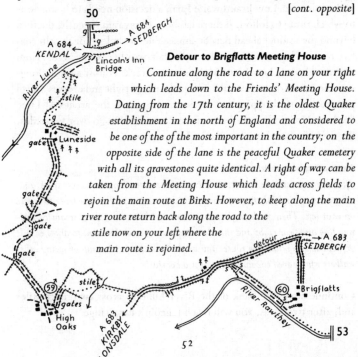

Detour to Brigflatts Meeting House

Continue along the road to a lane on your right which leads down to the Friends' Meeting House. Dating from the 17th century, it is the oldest Quaker establishment in the north of England and considered to be one of the of the most important in the country; on the opposite side of the lane is the peaceful Quaker cemetery with all its gravestones quite identical. A right of way can be taken from the Meeting House which leads across fields to rejoin the main route at Birks. However, to keep along the main river route return back along the road to the stile now on your left where the main route is rejoined.

Oaks Farm. Bear left to pass between the buildings through two gates leading to a green way. At the end of the enclosed way, keep right along the fence for a short distance and then bear left to cross over a stile and a tiny stream. Now follow the fence on your left which leads to a stile onto the A683. As well as looking out for cars, be careful of cyclists as this road section is part of the Cumbria Cycle Way. Turn left to follow the main road for under ½ mile to a stile on your right.

At this point a short detour of just over ½ mile is recommended to visit the Brigflatts Meeting House. However, if continuing straight on take the stile on your right which leads to the River Rawthey and, after another two stiles, towards Brigflatts Farm, the buildings of which are passed. The River Rawthey has its source 2,000 feet up on Baugh Fell.

BRIGFLATTS TO SEDBERGH

The river path is followed to stiles leading over the old railway line. Follow the river, crossing five stiles, until Birks Mill is reached. After passing Birks Mill, follow a narrow lane between houses at Birks. Take a gate on your right to rejoin the river. Follow the river, crossing two stiles, and then head away from the river to a third stile. After crossing this stile, head for a wood which is entered through a kissing-gate. The path swings to the right to a walled trench (not shown on the map) and, after leaving the wood at a stile, continues to a kissing-gate onto the road

just outside Sedbergh. If you are staying in the town, turn left and the centre is ½ mile away.

Sedbergh

Sedbergh (pronounced Sedber) is the main western entrance to the Yorkshire Dales and is just within the National Park boundary. It is an excellent base from which to explore the Dales and has a good range of accommodation, although no youth hostel. It is sheltered to the north by the Howgills and the outlook on three sides is of these fells. The main street has a number of alleys leading off it, one of which called Weavers Yard has an old house with a large chimney in which Bonnie Prince Charlie is said to have hidden after the 1745 rebellion.

Sedbergh is dominated by its public school which was founded in the early 16th century. The original 1716 building on the Dent road is now a library and museum. The fine looking church in the centre of the town has Norman origins and has a 15th-century tower.

The town has strong Quaker associations and George Fox preached in the district on many occasions, the most famous one at Firbank in 1652. Adam Sedgwick, an old boy of the school, was one of the country's earliest and best geologists and did much research in his own backyard. He was born in Dent village in 1785.

Sedbergh to Dentdale Youth Hostel

Distance: 11½ miles (12 miles including the deviation to Dent)
Going: Easy
Highest point: Dentdale Youth Hostel – 908 feet
Map required: O.S. Outdoor Leisure 2 Yorkshire Dales, Western area

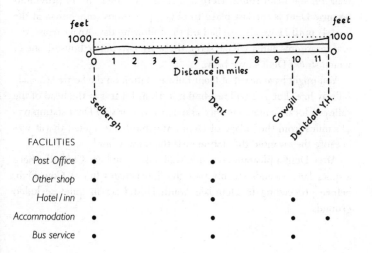

On this sixth day, the Dales Way is again followed, west to east, as far as Dentdale Youth Hostel. The walk traverses perhaps the most beautiful and most secluded of all the dales. Dentdale is isolated both by the hills which hem its eastern and western ends and by the narrowness of the roads that lead in and out of it. The traverse mostly follows the River Dee and its valley of lush fields with rounded fells on all sides.

There is no better way to arrive in Dentdale other than 'on foot' from the Irish Sea as a quiet and perceptive traveller now attuned to the beauty of the countryside. This valley tries to exclude the motor car with its narrow winding lanes but welcomes the walker with many delightful paths alongside the River Dee and its tributaries, and others leading onto the surrounding fells.

After leaving Sedbergh there are retrospective views to the Howgill Fells before enticing views ahead beckon you on to the hidden delights of Dentdale. With an easy day's walking ahead the opportunity should not be missed to visit the village of Dent which is only two minutes' walk off the main route. Here is a chance to stock up on provisions because Dent is the last place to obtain provisions (other than at the hostel) until Hawes is reached on the following day. Apart from several tea-rooms and a village shop, there are two public houses, one of which stocks Dent's own brew.

You might have heard of Dent railway station on the Settle–Carlisle railway line, but you will not find it in Dent for it is at the head of the valley. A local farmer was once asked by a visitor why Dent station was 4½ miles from the village of Dent. Apparently he replied that it was because they wanted the station near the railway line!

After Dent a pleasant riverside walk takes you near Cowgill where a quiet lane ascends steeply past the Sportsman's Inn at Cow Dub, before proceeding to Dentdale Youth Hostel set in quiet secluded grounds.

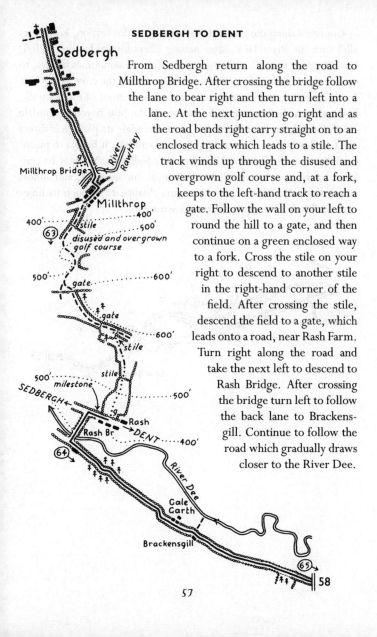

From Sedbergh return along the road to Millthrop Bridge. After crossing the bridge follow the lane to bear right and then turn left into a lane. At the next junction go right and as the road bends right carry straight on to an enclosed track which leads to a stile. The track winds up through the disused and overgrown golf course and, at a fork, keeps to the left-hand track to reach a gate. Follow the wall on your left to round the hill to a gate, and then continue on a green enclosed way to a fork. Cross the stile on your right to descend to another stile in the right-hand corner of the field. After crossing the stile, descend the field to a gate, which leads onto a road, near Rash Farm. Turn right along the road and take the next left to descend to Rash Bridge. After crossing the bridge turn left to follow the back lane to Brackensgill. Continue to follow the road which gradually draws closer to the River Dee.

57

Continue along the pleasant lane which, on this section, keeps parallel with the River Dee. After passing Ellers footbridge on the left, leave the road to head, across ground which can sometimes be wet, to the river and a stile. After crossing the stile, follow the river, going over five more stiles. The river is our companion for most of today's walk, flowing towards us as we walk. It rises in the hills beyond Dentdale Youth Hostel, on Blea Moor. In Upper Dentdale its passage is direct and fast-flowing but, on reaching Lower Dentdale, it begins to meander before joining the River Rawthey near Sedbergh. You may be confused by the river being full and flowing at one moment, and almost empty the next. This is when the water disappears through its limestone bed only to reappear further downstream.

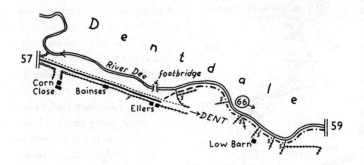

Cross another stile and then go through a gate, cross a second stile and then a footbridge. Barth Bridge is reached next: cross stiles either side of the road leading over the bridge, then continue alongside the river, as before. After six more stiles, the path joins the road briefly. At this point a short deviation can be made to Dent: *see* details page 60. However, if you do not wish to visit the village, continue to follow the riverside path, over five stiles, to reach Church Bridge. Go up a flight of steps to the road.

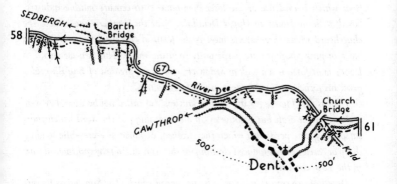

DENT TO COWGILL

Leave Church Bridge over a stile on the opposite side of the road. Go over another stile and cross a stream on your left. After crossing over a stile, follow the wall on your left leading back to the river.

Deviation to Dent

The village is reached by continuing along the road to your right for a few minutes. Dent is only a village in size but historically is known as Dent Town. Once a bustling community of close on 1800 people, it now has a permanent population of around a third of that figure. Access to Dent is not easy and this has helped to preserve its unique character. Narrow, winding streets are cobble-carpeted from wall to wall. Sturdy stone cottages sit snugly beneath low stone-pitched roofs of dark stone slabs. The township is well worthy of its status as a Conservation Area. The 15th-century Norman church has marble inlays in the floor which is evidence of the later dominant 19th-century marble industry, based at Stone House in Upper Dentdale. Near the southern entrance to the churchyard where three streets meet is the focus of the village, a rough-hewn block of pink Shap granite perpetually spouting water. This is a memorial to Dent's most famous son, Adam Sedgwick, one of the greatest of English geologists; his father was Dent's vicar in the 18th century.

Dent is also famous for its 'terrible knitters', so called not because they were useless at their craft but because of an older meaning of the word which indicated the great speed with which they worked, at home or even while tending sheep or cattle. They produced clothing for the army during the continental wars in the 18th century.

Dent has two traditional public houses one of which, The Sun, brews its very own Dent beer in a small brewery further along the route at Cowgill; however, don't drink too much as you may not get to Dentdale Youth Hostel 400 feet above the village!

The main route should be rejoined at Church Bridge by taking the small lane from the centre of the village that descends the valley to the bridge: see main route directions on previous page.

Follow the river to go over four stiles and through a gate then, when it turns away, continue along Deepdale Beck, crossing four stiles to reach Mill Bridge. Turn left along the road to cross Deepdale Beck and almost immediately take a stile on your left. Ascend to a viewpoint: there are excellent views from here including Whernside (2424ft) to the south-west and Great Coum (2254ft) to the south-east. Now descend to the river alongside a wall on your left. After going through a stile and gate, cross the Dee again at Tommy Bridge. Then turn right to cross a stile.

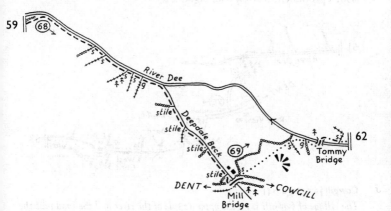

After the stile, continue to follow the Dee over three more stiles. Then cross the footbridge on your right and pass to the left of the confines of a ravine which is lined by trees. It is usually dry but water reappears just before the River Dee. Go over a stile, cross a stream and continue to a gate and a lane, where you turn left. After a short stretch, turn right along a stony track and then, in front of a large barn, take a gate on your left. Cross a small beck and stile, pass a barn to another stile, and reach a track leading past West Clint. Go through a gate, then over a stile crossing a small beck. Follow a fence and wall on your left with a prominent scar on your right.

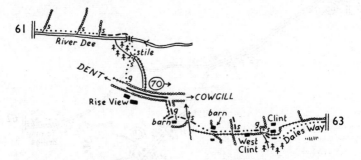

Cowgill [see page 64]

The village of Cowgill is on the opposite side of the river and the road past the village is called the Coal Road, and does indeed lead to an area of long-disused collieries on Widdale Fell, passing Dent station which, at 1,145 feet is the highest railway station in England. The Cowgill village chapel was the subject of an Act of Parliament in 1869. A new curate wanted to change the name from Cowgill Chapel to Kirkthwaite Chapel. However Adam Sedgwick was against this and wrote a pamphlet called: 'TO THE MEMORIAL OF THE TRUSTEES, COWGILL CHAPEL, 1868', arguing for the name to be retained. Queen Victoria saw the pamphlet since Sedgwick was then working with Prince Albert, reforming the teaching of science at universities throughout Britain. She summoned the Prime Minster and an Act of Parliament was passed to retain the original name of the chapel – the Cowgill Chapel Act 1869.

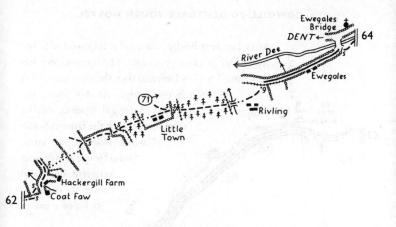

Take a stile on your left and cross a field to another stile. Cross over the stile and a beck and bear left along the access track before crossing a stile on your right. Continue to cross another stile and head for the access track. Head down it for a few yards and then branch right to cross a stile. The path descends to two stiles which lead into a plantation. Leave the plantation by a stile and cross the access track leading to Little Town on your right. Cross three stiles leading to another part of the plantation. Leave the plantation over a stile, cross a small beck and pass below the buildings of Rivling. Join an access track for a short distance but leave it to go through a gate onto a narrow lane. Turn right along the lane and pass Ewegales Farm. Just before Ewegales Bridge take the stile on the right.

Follow the river and, after two stiles, a narrow lane is reached at Lea Yeat Bridge: this leads to Cowgill.

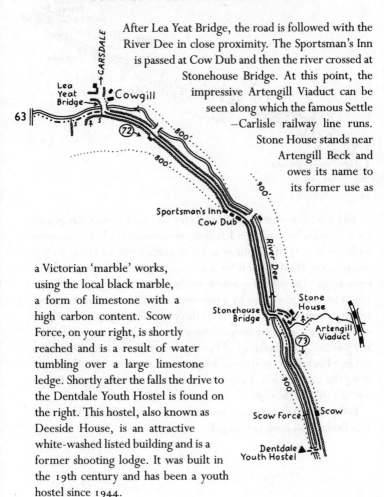

After Lea Yeat Bridge, the road is followed with the River Dee in close proximity. The Sportsman's Inn is passed at Cow Dub and then the river crossed at Stonehouse Bridge. At this point, the impressive Artengill Viaduct can be seen along which the famous Settle –Carlisle railway line runs. Stone House stands near Artengill Beck and owes its name to its former use as

a Victorian 'marble' works, using the local black marble, a form of limestone with a high carbon content. Scow Force, on your right, is shortly reached and is a result of water tumbling over a large limestone ledge. Shortly after the falls the drive to the Dentdale Youth Hostel is found on the right. This hostel, also known as Deeside House, is an attractive white-washed listed building and is a former shooting lodge. It was built in the 19th century and has been a youth hostel since 1944.

Dentdale Youth Hostel to Hawes Youth Hostel

Distance: 12 miles (16 miles including the detour to Hardraw Force)
Going: Moderate
Highest point: Cam High Road – 1,930 feet
Map required: O.S. Outdoor Leisure 2 Yorkshire Dales, Western area

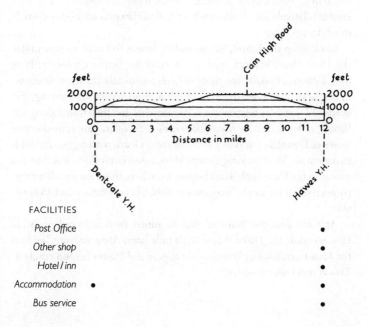

FACILITIES	
Post Office	•
Other shop	•
Hotel / inn	•
Accommodation	• •
Bus service	•

Railway enthusiasts and those who love the high open fells will enjoy today. For the former there is the Dent Head and Ribblehead viaducts to admire, while for the latter the 'Three Peaks' of Whernside, Ingleborough and Pen-y-ghent can be seen as the Pennine watershed is crossed. However, don't forget your warm clothing or suntan lotion (depending on the time of year) as the Roman Cam High Road and West Cam Road, at over 1,800 feet, have a reputation for cold winds for half the year and skin-burning winds for the other half. Also don't forget your packed lunch and drinks as there are no opportunities to buy refreshments along the way. You will be glad to know that if it has rained throughout the walk so far, it should stop today as, on crossing Stoops Moss, North Yorkshire is entered, a county recognised as being much drier than Cumbria. On this seventh day, the distance to be covered is relatively low, but an early arrival in Hawes is advised as there is much to see there.

On leaving the hostel, the ascending lane is followed to pass under the Dent Head Viaduct over which runs the Settle–Carlisle railway line. Constructionally the most difficult, scenically the most dramatic in England, it follows the Vale of Eden to go across Mallerstang, the heads of Dentdale, Garsdale and Wensleydale and then down along the Ribble valley to Settle. Above the viaduct, there are fine retrospective views of Dentdale – a valley you will always leave with regret and wish to return to. After crossing Stoops Moss, a descent follows and then the ascent to the Cam High Road begins; from here there are excellent retrospective views to the magnificent Ribblehead Viaduct and Whernside.

At Cam End the Pennine Way is joined (and followed as far as Hawes) while the Dales Way is left a mile later. After skirting Ten End the broad expanses of Wensleydale appear and Hawes is soon reached. This is real Dales country.

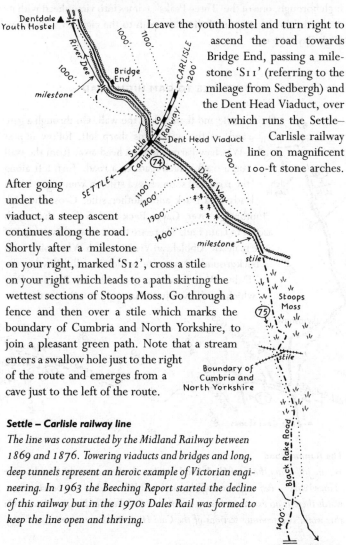

Leave the youth hostel and turn right to ascend the road towards Bridge End, passing a milestone 'S11' (referring to the mileage from Sedbergh) and the Dent Head Viaduct, over which runs the Settle–Carlisle railway line on magnificent 100-ft stone arches.

After going under the viaduct, a steep ascent continues along the road. Shortly after a milestone on your right, marked 'S12', cross a stile on your right which leads to a path skirting the wettest sections of Stoops Moss. Go through a fence and then over a stile which marks the boundary of Cumbria and North Yorkshire, to join a pleasant green path. Note that a stream enters a swallow hole just to the right of the route and emerges from a cave just to the left of the route.

Settle – Carlisle railway line

The line was constructed by the Midland Railway between 1869 and 1876. Towering viaducts and bridges and long, deep tunnels represent an heroic example of Victorian engineering. In 1963 the Beeching Report started the decline of this railway but in the 1970s Dales Rail was formed to keep the line open and thriving.

The path leads to a fork with a track before High Gayle Farm. Here, Ingleborough, one of the 'Three Peaks', comes into view ahead with its distinctive broad summit. Follow the path to the right to walk above High Gayle Farm.

HIGH GAYLE TO CAM HIGH ROAD

Cross a stile and then follow the wall. Go through a gate and, as the wall turns sharp left, follow it past Winshaw Farm and then head away from the wall on a track which leads to a road. Turn left along the road and soon cross a stile on your right which leads to a track and another stile. Cross the high footbridge over Gayle Beck and follow the rough ascent to Cam End. There are fine retrospective views of the majestic Ribblehead Viaduct, with Whernside in its background. Our route, which is still following the Dales Way, here merges with the Pennine Way which is followed until Hawes, 7½ miles further on.

The Roman Road
We are following the Cam High Road which is the Roman road from where the 'Three Peaks' – Pen-y-ghent, Ingleborough and Whernside – may be seen. East-wards there is an expansive view towards the bleak head of Langstrothdale. On this walk, two separate sections of the Cam High Road are covered, both very

straight in the manner of Roman road construction. This section was once called the Devil's Causeway, in the belief that no human hands could have engineered such a road so well, or one for so long. In the Middle Ages, men feared nightfall on the Cam High Road. They hastened onwards, glad to hear the sound of Bainbridge's horn carried to them on the wind. Wolves roamed the tops and the hornblower sounded the alarm as a warning for all shepherds to bring down their sheep and cattle to safety. The other section of the Cam High Road that we follow is beyond Hawes on the next day's walking.

CAM HIGH ROAD TO KIDHOW GATE

After leaving Cam End, bear north-east over Cam Fell in the footsteps of the Roman legions that once marched this way. Just after a stile in a wall, the Dales Way path continues to the right, passing Oughtershaw and Wharfedale on its way to finish at Ilkley. It has been a good companion for 40 miles.

Cam High Road (Roman road)
70
80
limestone clints
1800'
1800'
gate
1700'
signpost
79
stile → Dales Way
1600'
1700'
1600'
1500'
Cam High Road (Roman road)
1500'
Cam Fell

Our route stays with the Pennine Way, passing through a gate and maintaining height. Weather conditions at this exposed altitude of around 1,800 feet can be fierce and you will certainly notice it if you get caught in a cold easterly wind.

68

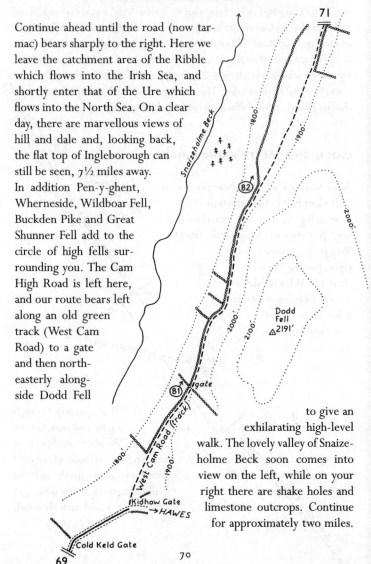

Continue ahead until the road (now tarmac) bears sharply to the right. Here we leave the catchment area of the Ribble which flows into the Irish Sea, and shortly enter that of the Ure which flows into the North Sea. On a clear day, there are marvellous views of hill and dale and, looking back, the flat top of Ingleborough can still be seen, 7½ miles away. In addition Pen-y-ghent, Wherneside, Wildboar Fell, Buckden Pike and Great Shunner Fell add to the circle of high fells surrounding you. The Cam High Road is left here, and our route bears left along an old green track (West Cam Road) to a gate and then northeasterly alongside Dodd Fell

to give an exhilarating high-level walk. The lovely valley of Snaizeholme Beck soon comes into view on the left, while on your right there are shake holes and limestone outcrops. Continue for approximately two miles.

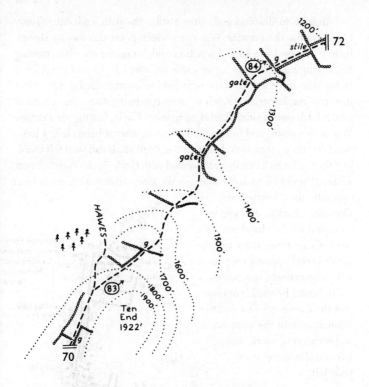

After a gate, the West Cam Road (track) takes a left fork and drops down to woods seen below. Do not take this path but take the right fork which runs along the flank of Ten End, where there are ancient rights of peat cutting. The fork is marked by stones and a signpost Pennine Way. If you find yourself descending to woods, you are wrong and must retrace your steps. The correct way forward soon starts to descend and on a clear day Wensleydale and eventually Hawes come into view. Follow the clear path to go through four gates and over a stile.

Continue to descend and, after a stile, the path leads into Gaudy Lane. Follow the Pennine Way signs which point the way to Hawes. Follow Gaudy Lane to a T-junction and, immediately after turning right along a narrow lane, cross a stile on your left. Cross the field to a facing stile and then cross the next field to another facing stile. After this stile immediately turn left to cross two more stiles, the second of which leads onto a lane. Turn right to enter Gayle, leaving the Pennine Way at this point, and follow the lane until, after it bends left, a junction is reached. Turn right for just a couple of yards and then left to follow the road which briefly runs parallel with Gayle Beck. Turn left over a stile (if you wish to avoid stiles, *see* the alternative road route below) opposite the Wensleydale Creamery. Fork to the right to go round the left-hand side of a barn. Cross three stiles and the youth hostel appears on your left. Alternatively, to reach the youth hostel by road, continue past the Creamery, descend to a T-junction with the main street and turn left to a fork. Keep left and the hostel is on your left.

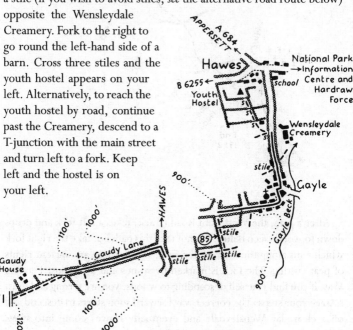

The detour to Hardraw Force

Hawes is an ideal location to have a rest day since there is so much to see, not least nearby Hardraw Force. A visit there amounts to a round trip from the youth hostel of 4 miles and, although it is not included in the main route, do not miss it. If you do not have time for a rest day, at least visit the falls when you arrive.

From the youth hostel, follow the main street to cross Gayle Beck to reach the National Park Information Centre. Follow the Pennine Way by taking the road left adjoining the Centre. Either follow the road which, in due course, crosses the River Ure, or cut off a corner by passing through a stile (signposted Pennine Way) on your left. At a gate, rejoin the road and cross the bridge over the River Ure. Ignore a first footpath sign to Hardraw, but where the road ascends take a stile on your left to follow the path which leads across fields, and over several stiles and gates, to Hardraw. The path enters the hamlet opposite the church and Green Dragon Inn. The Pennine Way continues over the bridge and then diverts north-west heading for Great Shunner Fell; we shall not meet it again on our route.

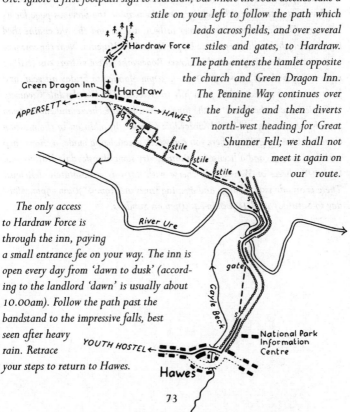

The only access to Hardraw Force is through the inn, paying a small entrance fee on your way. The inn is open every day from 'dawn to dusk' (according to the landlord 'dawn' is usually about 10.00am). Follow the path past the bandstand to the impressive falls, best seen after heavy rain. Retrace your steps to return to Hawes.

Hawes

The market town of Hawes lies 850 feet above sea level with high fells to both the north and south sweeping up a further 1,000 feet. Hawes enjoyed a boom in the 1870s when the railway line came up the dale and was linked to the Settle – Carlisle line at Hawes junction, later renamed Garsdale. Although many of the buildings date from the late Victorian period, they are interspersed around the Market Place and the Old Bridge with houses of the 17th and 18th centuries. Hawes received its market charter in 1700 although no record of settlement exists until 1307. It is now the commercial and market centre of Upper Wensleydale with a good range of shops and accommodation.

It is a good idea to visit the National Park Information Centre to see their displays and obtain local knowledge; see the map on the previous page for its location. The Centre is in the former railway station and the old engine shed house nearby houses the impressive Upper Dales Folk Museum. Near the entrance to the car park is the remarkable Hawes Ropeworks where visitors can still see ropes being made. It is open 9.00am–5.30pm Monday to Friday all year, and from 10.00am on Saturdays from July to October. The Wensleydale Creamery in Gayle Lane is the 'home' of the famous Wensleydale cheese and the museum portrays the history of "Real Wensleydale Cheese". In addition to the museum there is a viewing gallery where you can watch cheese being made, a cheese shop with free tasting, and a licensed restaurant. Try some Wensleydale Wallace and Gromit™ cheese or Wensleydale cheese with apricots – absolutely delicious! There is an admission charge and opening times are from 9.30am–5pm, Monday to Saturday, and 10.00am–4.30pm on Sundays.

Hawes Youth Hostel to Aysgarth Falls Youth Hostel

Distance: 13 miles
Going: Strenuous then easy
Highest point: Cam High Road – 1,850 feet
Map required: O. S. Outdoor Leisure 30 Yorkshire Dales, Northern
and Central areas

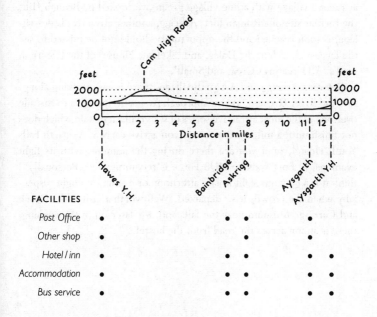

There are a number of villages on this section of the walk, with excellent shops and public houses, so obviating the need to carry other than basic emergency provisions.

Today's walk involves an initial steep climb of nearly 1,000 feet from Hawes to the Roman Cam High Road, passing between the fells of Drumaldace at 2,015 feet and Yorburgh at 1,700 feet. This high-level route gives extensive views of Wensleydale, the quieter and secluded Raydale, and Semer Water; the latter is one of the few large expanses of water in the Yorkshire Dales. Although not of the stature of the Lake District lakes, Semer Water has a beautiful setting, especially when viewed from today's route.

A gentle descent to Bainbridge alongside the River Bain gives you the chance to recover from earlier exertions. Bainbridge is a very attractive village with a fine village green overlooked by Brough Hill, the former site of a Roman fort. Askrigg, another attractive Dales village, is soon reached and the opportunity should not be missed to see the largest church in the Dales, and 'Skeldale House' of the television series 'All Creatures Great and Small'.

Between Askrigg and Aysgarth villages there is easy walking alongside the River Ure and, as you approach Aysgarth, it begins to cascade over one of the most attractive series of waterfalls in Britain which does not finish until a mile further on. If you arrive early at Aysgarth Falls Youth Hostel, or if you are there during the summer with its light evenings, a short walk to High Force is recommended. Personally, I think it is a glorious sight in late afternoon or evening sunlight, especially when the crowds have departed. Well worth a visit is the Coach and Carriage Museum near the falls and, for later on in the evening, there is an inn across the road from the hostel.

From the youth hostel retrace the route to the bridge over Gayle Beck
which will now be on your left. Cross the bridge
and turn right along the road. After a few houses
on the left, cross a stile, also on your left. Head to
the stile across the field and then go over another stile.
Immediately turn right over another stile leading
to Shaw Lane and then immediately turn left
to follow the enclosed path up
the hill. The path turns sharp left
to go through a gate. It then bears right
over rocks to ascend to another gate. At a third
gate, the now indistinct path bears right to
ascend steeply to a stile next to a gate.
Continue to ascend to where another
path joins Blackburn Sike. Cross over
the Sike and bear right to ascend to a
gap in the middle of
the facing wall. The

path, still indis-
tinct, climbs very
steeply half-left to a
wall gap on the left.
Continue ahead to go
through another wall gap.
The path becomes clear and
bears left to a stile and gate in
the wall to the left. After the
stile, turn right along the bridleway and
follow it to a gap in a facing wall. Bear
left (to the line of the wall), ignoring the
tracks ahead and bending to the right, and
continue to go through another wall gap.

Map labels: Hawes Youth Hostel; 86; Gayle; BAINBRIDGE; 900'; Gayle Beck; SLEDDALE; stiles; 1000'; 1100'; 1200'; 1300'; 1400'; 1500'; Blackburn Sike; stile; 87; gate and stile; 1600'; 1700'; 1800'

78

Continue ahead and cross a stile to reach the Cam High Road. This stony track takes very little traffic and only the occasional farm vehicle uses it. The road continues left to Bainbridge but, in search of Semer Water, our route crosses straight over the track to cross a stile on the other side.

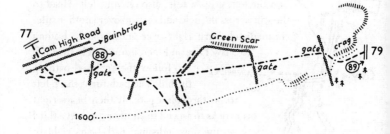

CAM HIGH ROAD TO BAINBRIDGE

Almost immediately turn left onto a bridleway which crosses the path. Follow this to go through a gate. The path bends left and right to go through a wall gap. Continue ahead to go through another wall gap, ignoring tracks and paths to both left and right, and then go through a gate. Maintain height to another gate. The path starts a steep descent between crags on the left and woods on the right; however, pause for a moment to look at Semer Water on the right which is best viewed from here.

Semer Water
It is thought that Iron Age lake-dwellings once existed at Semer Water; it is now a popular venue for a variety of water sports. The side valley containing Semer Water has no satisfactory name, although Semerdale is sometimes used. Above the lake it is generally referred to as Raydale, this being the central, the longest and the only level one of the three valleys which merge between Marsett and Stalling Busk, two villages to the immediate south-west of Semer Water; Bardale and Cragdale are the lesser two.

There are fine views ahead of Addlebrough which, at 1,561 feet, is a fine flat-topped fell. Go through three gates leading onto a minor lane at a sharp bend. Turn left to ascend the lane to join the Cam High Road again (a short cut across rough grassland can be taken by crossing the stile on your right which leads to another stile onto the road). The Roman road has travelled across the head of Sleddale while you have been enjoying the delights of Hawes. Turn right onto the Cam High Road and follow it for just over a mile; from the road there are extensive views of the broad sweep of Wensleydale.

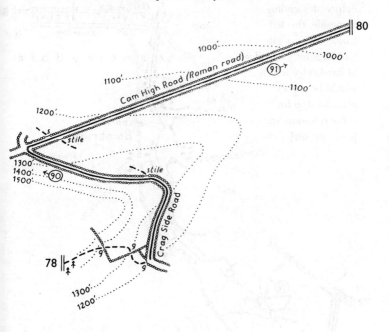

On reaching a tarmac lane, turn right onto it and ascend along the road to Gill Edge. Do not follow the road right but instead go along the farm drive through two gates, then cross a stile found on your left. Head down the field to another stile at the bottom, across a second field to another stile. Then follow a sketchy path leading across a third field to a wall gap. Having passed a barn on your left, a clearer path now leads to a gap between a wall and fence and the way continues to a stile and then a third wall gap above the River Bain before descending alongside the left-hand wall to a gate. Continue into the village of Bainbridge which would be a good place to stop for some refreshment.

[*cont. opposite*]

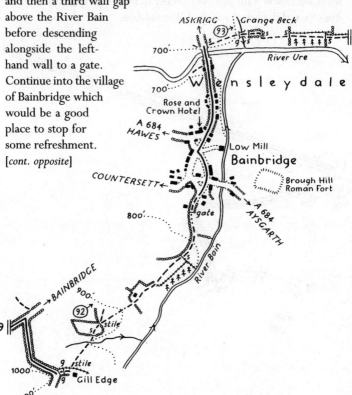

Bainbridge

The Romans came to Bainbridge in about AD 80 and established a succession of forts on Brough Hill, a grassy hillock to the east of the village, occupying the site almost continuously for over 300 years. At the centre of the village green, medieval stocks are a reminder of past punishment and were still in use in Queen Elizabeth I's time.

Although the Rose and Crown overlooking the green is dated 1445 (above the front door), its present appearance suggests an early 19th-century building. Low Mill on the east side of the green has been restored, together with its fine water-wheels; it exhibits dolls' houses which can also be made to order. Access to the mill is by appointment. The River Bain, on which the mill is sited, drains from Semer Water into a steep two-mile course, entering Bainbridge over a fine cas-cade of waterfalls above the main road. It then flows down the eastern edge of the village into the River Ure. If you wish to have a closer look at what is some-times regarded as England's shortest named river turn right along the A684 and cross the bridge.

BAINBRIDGE TO ASKRIGG

[*see* opposite] From the village green head north on the road to Askrigg and cross the bridge over the River Ure. Immediately take a stile on your right and go diagonally across a field to a gated bridge over Grange Beck which leads to another stile and to the dismantled railway line. The path goes over another stile and then runs parallel with the River Ure to go over a third stile. After passing a wood on your right, a fourth stile is reached. Cross this and follow the fence on your left.

After another stile, turn left to reach the road into Askrigg. Turn right and follow it until a track on your right is reached prior to the house with the double garage. A brief visit to the centre of Askrigg is recommended; do not, therefore, turn down the track but continue straight into the village [*see* opposite].

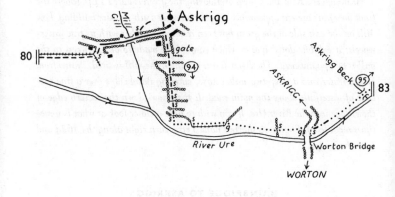

ASKRIGG TO AYSGARTH FALLS YOUTH HOSTEL

Retrace your steps from the centre of Askrigg and turn left along the track down past the animal feed works. From the gate at the bottom pass between the ramparts of a former railway bridge and continue in the same direction through a series of five stiles. From the last a sketchy path heads straight for the river but, instead of following it to the bank, turn left on a low embankment to reach a stile in a wall corner. Follow a fence away from it (parallel with the river) to a gate from where the river bank is at last joined. Accompany the Ure downstream to cross over a stile and soon emerge, at a gate, onto a road adjacent to the char-acterless Worton Bridge. Cross a stile opposite and continue down the river to a footbridge over Askrigg Beck.

Askrigg

Most houses in Askrigg date from the 18th and 19th centuries, the period of the village's increasing prosperity through its clock-making, lead mining and textile industries. The Richmond–Lancaster Turnpike which came through the village in 1751, also was a major influence.

The main street widens near the 15th-century parish church and has as a focal-point an iron bullring in the cobbles. The church is the largest and the most imposing in Wensleydale and the nave roof is one of the finest, if not the finest in North Yorkshire. Opposite is Cringley House, the 'Skeldale House' of the BBC television series 'All Creatures Great and Small'. This was the surgery-home of Siegfried Farnon, his brother Tristan, and James and Helen Herriot. Through his books and later the films and television series, James Herriot became the world's most famous vet; he died in 1995.

Go through a gate and over a second footbridge leading to a gate near the buildings of Nappa Mill Farm. Take the farm drive up to the left but

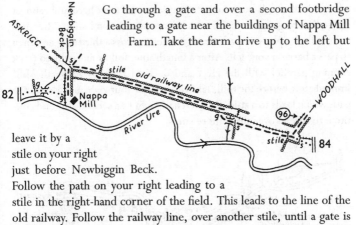

leave it by a
stile on your right
just before Newbiggin Beck.
Follow the path on your right leading to a
stile in the right-hand corner of the field. This leads to the line of the old railway. Follow the railway line, over another stile, until a gate is reached on your right, just before a small beck. After going through the gate, keep left to cross the small stiled footbridge over the beck. Follow the fence on your left, leading to a stile to pass the farm track from Woodhall, then continue ahead to cross another stile.

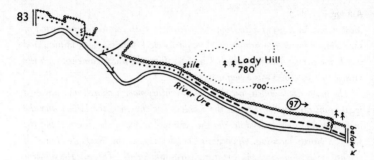

The path follows the river, crossing four stiles, until a gate is reached leading on to a lane. Go over the long narrow footbridge. The lane joins the A684 at a T-junction. Turn left, taking care of passing traffic, and continue along the road for approximately ½ mile until you reach a break in the wall on your left. You leave the road here and, almost immediately, go over a stile which leads to a second stile. After this stile, follow a pleasant path through trees to cross a third stile and then to pass a barn on your left. After a fourth stile, follow an enclosed track running parallel with the river and descend towards Aysgarth Mill. Immediately before the mill, take the gate on your right and ascend the path which leads to a stile. Proceed half-right to a second stile and continue to ascend over three more stiles.

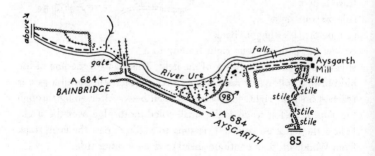

After crossing another stile, go through a narrow gap between houses leading to the village of Aysgarth. The village is in two parts with the youth hostel and waterfalls over ½ mile further on [see page 86]. It would be sensible to do any shopping in the first half of the village before the final leg of the day's walk.

To reach the youth hostel, turn left towards the Methodist Church along a back lane which leads to a gate. The path rises at first and then generally keeps level to go through a multitude of identical stiles across fields. When a road is finally met, turn right and the youth hostel is soon reached on the left.

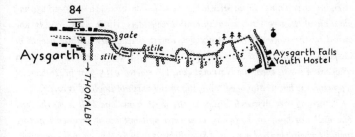

Aysgarth and Aysgarth Falls [*see* page 89 for the map]

As mentioned in the introduction to this eighth day, the best time to see the spectacular Aysgarth Falls is towards the end of the day when all the tourists have gone, or during the long summer evenings. You can of course save the waterfalls for the next day, when the route passes by two of them and, instead, visit some of the other sites which stay open fairly late.

From the youth hostel and the church, a short, steep hill descends to the river, crosses by a narrow stone bridge, and climbs the northern bank where you will see the National Park Information Centre. However, pause as you cross the bridge since, to your left, you will see High Force in the most beautiful setting. The River Ure, confined between wooded banks, falls over a series of broad, shallow terraces extending over a mile. To see Middle Force and Lower Force, you will need to sample a bit of the next day's route through Freeholders' Wood. This wood is now owned by the National Park Authority, but its freeholders, mainly people in Carperby, retain certain common rights including that of gathering wood. In co-operation with them the National Park has started a 15-year programme of coppicing the hazel. Managed coppicing in the north of England is rare.

Returning over Aysgarth Bridge to the south bank Yore Mill is on the left. The mill was built in 1784–85 as a corn mill but has a chequered history including being burned down in 1853. Rebuilt to twice the original size it subsequently had a variety of uses; between 1912 and 1959 it was a flour mill. Since 1967 its roomy interior has housed the Yorkshire Carriage Museum which has a fascinating variety of old coaches and carriages, as well as an unequalled view of High Force. The museum is open 9.30am–8pm every day from April to October. From November to March it is open from 9.30am to dusk.

Further up the hill, again on the left, is St Andrew's church. Although it was largely rebuilt in 1866, its 4½-acre churchyard indicates its earlier importance as the mother-church for the whole of Upper Wensleydale. Inside the church the exquisite wooden screen filling the south side of the chancel was brought to Aysgarth from Jervaulx Abbey at the Dissolution of the Monasteries. It was carved in about 1506 by members of the famous Ripon School of Carvers. At its western end is the delicately carved Vicar's Stall made from two bench-ends from Jervaulx.

Aysgarth Falls Youth Hostel to Ellingstring Youth Hostel

Distance: 16 miles

Going: Easy

Highest point: Castle Bolton – 800 feet

Map required: O. S. Outdoor Leisure 30 Yorkshire Dales, Northern & Central areas, O. S. Pathfinder 630 Middleham & Jervaulx Abbey

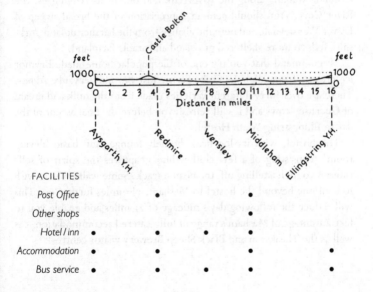

FACILITIES

	Aysgarth Y.H.	Redmire	Wensley	Middleham	Ellingstring Y.H.
Post Office		•		•	
Other shops				•	
Hotel / inn	•		•	•	
Accommodation	•	•		•	
Bus service	•	•	•	•	•

As with the previous day there are a number of villages on the route, most of which have shops and/or public houses, so it is not necessary to carry other than basic provisions.

Although the daily mileage increases today, the walking is over relatively flat pleasant countryside and good progress can be made. At Hollins House you have reached the half-way point of the walk; only another 100 miles to go! There is plenty to see *en route* with Aysgarth's waterfalls and Bolton Castle soon being reached. After the village of Redmire, Bolton Hall is passed and then Wensley is reached; if open its fine church should be visited – it is a gem. A few miles further on comes Middleham and I guarantee few will be able to resist the temptation of the castle. With Jervaulx Abbey also to be visited, a good pace needs to be set throughout the day.

To complement the interesting buildings on the route, there is fine riverside walking along the River Ure and one of its tributaries, the River Cover. You should gain an appreciation of the broad sweep of Lower Wensleydale and note the change from the harsher upland Yorkshire fells to more sheltered grassland and arable farmland.

I recommend that you try one of the popular home-made Brymor ice-creams from High Jervaulx Farm, just beyond Jervaulx Abbey. There are over forty different varieties made from the milk and cream of Guernsey cows and it will refresh you before the final ascent of the day to Ellingstring Youth Hostel.

The hostel, with its log fires, homely lounge, and basic 'drying room' (consisting of a few clothes lines) captures the spirit of self-catered youth hostelling off the beaten track. Some walkers may wish to continue beyond the hostel to Masham, 5½ miles further on. This will reduce the following day's mileage of 21 miles and enable you to take advantage of Masham's range of fully-catered accommodation – as well as the Theakston and Black Sheep Brewery visitor centres!

From the youth hostel, head back towards the church and descend to the bridge to cross the River Ure, not forgetting to have a final look at High Force to your left. Follow the road round to the right and where it turns left go through a gate on your right into Freeholders' Wood. Middle Force is soon reached just off to your right; it is an impressive sight, especially after heavy rain. Continue along the woodland path and, after a gate, the path briefly leaves the trees. Follow the descending path to your right and go through another gate to lead through trees until Lower Force is reached. A few yards past Lower Force ignore a path ascending left and follow the path ahead which soon bears left, over a stile, to leave the river. At a fence turn right heading towards another stile. After crossing the stile continue straight across the sloping field to a gate which leads between the buildings at Hollins House. After another gate follow the farm track away from the house. When the track bears left, head slightly right across the field to a stile. This leads to another field; now strike half-right over the brow to a gate in the far corner. The next section of the walk may not be correctly marked as a right of way on all Ordnance Survey maps – but has been double checked and confirmed as an Unclassified Road and is well signposted. After passing through the gate follow the wall on your left.

90

Halfway! 100

Hollins House

600'

500'

→CARPERBY

stile

Freeholders' Wood

River Ure

Lower Force

Middle Force

500'

High Force

Yorkshire Carriage Museum

600'

99

Aysgarth Falls Youth Hostel

Pass through another gate and cross a stile. Then follow the wall around to the right and head for a stile in the corner of the field. After crossing the stile follow an enclosed way to an extremely wet junction leading to a pleasant green byway (Thoresby Lane) which is followed all the way to a gate just before Low Thoresby Farm. Pass the farm on your right to go over a bridge. Leave the track immediately by going over a stile (in poor condition when last visited) in a fence on your left and then keep ahead over another stile in a wall. Head right towards a barn in the middle of the field. Carry on to pass another barn and then bear left to a stile leading to a road. Cross the road in a left and right 'dog-leg' to a lane.

[see opposite] Walk up the lane for ½ mile to Castle Bolton; note the fine views of the castle ahead and shortly to your left.

Bolton Castle

The castle was erected by the first Lord Scrope, Chancellor of England, in 1379, more as a fortified manor house with the needs of comfort predominating over those of defence. Designed with a huge four-storey tower some 100 feet high at each corner, four ranges of living quarters enclosing a courtyard and turrets in the middle of each of the two longer sides, it took eighteen years to complete. The antiquary Leland, writing in about 1546, asserted that it cost £12,000 to build, a sum equivalent to around £1.5 million today.

From July 1568 until January 1569 Mary, Queen of Scots was imprisoned at Bolton — apparently in some degree of comfort since about twenty servants were billeted in the village. The castle was garrisoned for the Royalists during the Civil War, besieged by the Parliamentary forces in 1645 and eventually surrendered. Two years later it was partially dismantled and in 1761 the north-east tower, weakened a century earlier, fell during a great storm. The other three towers survive almost to their original height. Owned by Lord Bolton, the castle has a museum of local history exhibits, and an excellent tea room. It has been considerably restored in recent years, with grant aid from English Heritage and is open from 10am–5pm every day from March to November.

CASTLE BOLTON TO WENSLEY

From the castle walk through the village and, as the road bears slightly left at the end of the village, take a track on your right. Here begins a multi-stiled section. The track descends steeply to a stile and, shortly afterwards, another stile is crossed on your left. Descend to the corner of the field to cross a third stile. Continue to descend to the corner of the next field to cross a fourth stile and then over a small bridge leading to a fifth stile and the dismantled railway. Cross over the railway to a sixth stile.

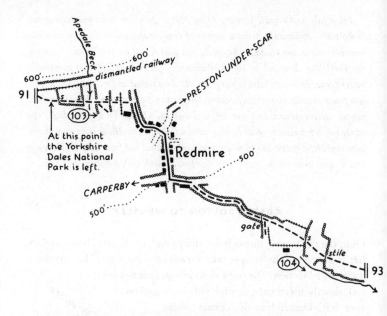

Bear left and at this point the Yorkshire Dales National Park is left, but do not despair as there is some fine walking country ahead and the North York Moors National Park to look forward to. Cross over a stile and then follow the wall on your right to a stile leading to Apedale Beck. There is no bridge and after heavy rain the only way to cross is on stones in the stream. Carry straight on over two stiles to a lane leading to Redmire. Turn right down the lane which then bends left. At a fork bear right to join another lane leading south to Carperby. Where this lane turns sharply right take the access lane to your left, then, after a house, take the enclosed track on your right. Follow the track as it gradually descends to a gate. Pass through the gate, ignore the path to your right, and head diagonally across a large field to a stile in the corner. Cross this and then bear slightly right to go over another.

Carry on more or less straight ahead, over three more stiles, until West Wood comes into view. Head up the slope to a kissing-gate leading into woods. Once in the woods carry straight on along a well-defined track. A viewpoint to the River Ure and Penhill in the far distance is passed in a clearing of trees on your right. The track descends to a gate in another clearing. Carry straight on to another gate where a line of trees comes up to the track. This track is tarmacked to Wensley village and is easy to follow by continuing straight on.

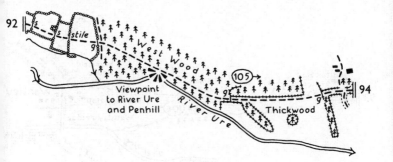

Bolton Hall is passed on your left: this was built by Charles Powlett who became the Duke of Bolton in 1678. The present Bolton Hall is largely a 1902 rebuilding after a serious fire but the shell of the 17th-century house remains. It is not open to visitors. Cross a footbridge over a beck and continue along the tarmacked track, passing Middle Lodge on your right. Eventually the A684 running through Wensley village is reached; turn right onto it and walk down the road and into the centre of the village.

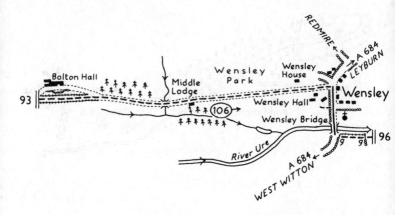

WENSLEY TO MIDDLEHAM

After crossing Wensley Bridge at the south end of the village go imme-diately through a gate on your left, then carry straight on along a track to another gate.

Wensley

This is a small village of 19th-century estate houses set round a neat green. On the hillsides above the village cattle and sheep predominate, whilst below are the first arable fields in the dale. For a century after 1202, when it received its charter, Wensley had the only market in the dale and this continued to function until the 16th century, although on a decreasing scale as other markets were established.

Plague struck Wensley in 1563 and, as the parish register notes: 'This year nothing set down.' Some surviving villagers fled to higher ground at Leyburn. The fortunes of Wensley was revived when Bolton Hall was built.

Wensley's church of the Holy Trinity is one of the finest in the Dales. Much of it dates from around 1300 but the tower was rebuilt in 1719. The interior is rich in furnishings and of particular interest are the traces of an early 14th-century wall painting, the 17th-century box-pews, a reliquary, a poor box, a two-decker pulpit and stalls with poppy-heads. The Scrope family pew includes part of a fine wood screen which probably came from Easby Abbey when it was dissolved in 1537, the abbey having been owned by the Scrope family. There is also a banner of the Loyal Dales Volunteers which was raised against Napoleon. The church was the setting for the television marriage of James and Helen Herriot.

Now follow the path which has been diverted to follow closely along the River Ure. The green pecked path on the Ordnance Survey map should be ignored and the river path followed instead. Where a swathe of trees appears on the right of the path, go through a gate, and then through another when a second swathe of trees is passed shortly thereafter. Where the river bends to the left, go through another gate and turn right to follow the edge of the field until a track is reached. Turn left along the track.

Middleham

Middleham is one of the north's great centres for racehorse training, a tradition going back two centuries. Beautiful horses on their way to the gallops outside the town are a common and delightful sight. The Swine Cross commemorates Richard's 1479 ratification of the Market Charter given to the town a century earlier by Ralph Neville, Earl of Westmorland. A lane nearby leads to St Mary and St Alkelda's church, dating mainly from the 13th and 14th centuries, and made a collegiate foundation by Richard in 1478. At some point during the last century, the writer Charles Kingsley was its canon. Kingsley House, the rectory next to the church, was built in 1752.

The first castle, its site marked by hawthorns, was built in the early Norman period. Its successor of 1170 passed into the hands of the Nevilles of Raby a century later but saw its great days during the War of the Roses. The castle remained Crown property until 1625, when it passed into private hands; it is now in the guardianship of English Heritage. It is open daily from 10am–6pm April to September, and from 10am–4pm in October.

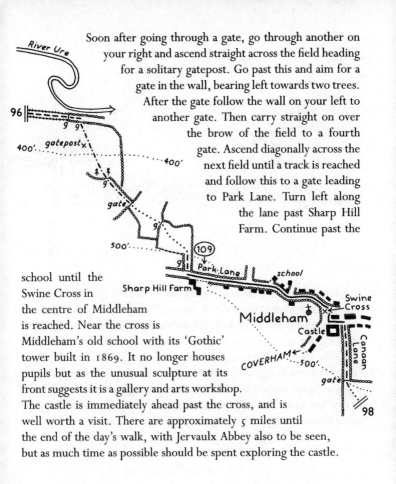

Soon after going through a gate, go through another on your right and ascend straight across the field heading for a solitary gatepost. Go past this and aim for a gate in the wall, bearing left towards two trees. After the gate follow the wall on your left to another gate. Then carry straight on over the brow of the field to a fourth gate. Ascend diagonally across the next field until a track is reached and follow this to a gate leading to Park Lane. Turn left along the lane past Sharp Hill Farm. Continue past the school until the Swine Cross in the centre of Middleham is reached. Near the cross is Middleham's old school with its 'Gothic' tower built in 1869. It no longer houses pupils but as the unusual sculpture at its front suggests it is a gallery and arts workshop. The castle is immediately ahead past the cross, and is well worth a visit. There are approximately 5 miles until the end of the day's walk, with Jervaulx Abbey also to be seen, but as much time as possible should be spent exploring the castle.

MIDDLEHAM TO ELLINGSTRING YOUTH HOSTEL

Turn left at the castle and then right into Canaan Lane. Carry on past the castle to the end of the lane and go through a gate. Cross the gradually sloping field diagonally left.

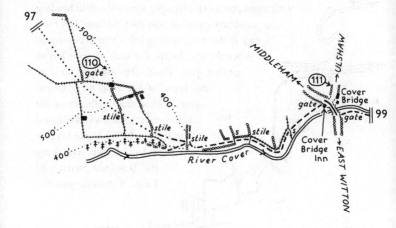

Keep heading diagonally across this large field to a gate in the corner and then continue in the same direction. Eventually a section of stone wall is reached with a stile in it. After crossing this, continue diagonally until another stile is reached at the corner of the next field. Continue along the fence, with trees on the right and then ahead to a stile. Then follow the path alongside the River Cover, crossing over three stiles, to a gate adjacent to the Cover Bridge Inn. Turn right to cross over Cover Bridge and then, by going through a gate on your left, follow the path along the river.

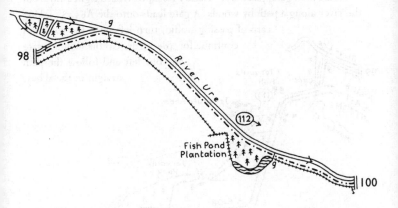

Shortly, the confluence of the Rivers Cover and Ure and another gate are reached. Follow the river bank for a mile to go through a gate at Fish Pond Plantation. At this point, the River Ure is sluggish although, after heavy rain, it is prone to flooding. The river rises some distance away beyond Hawes, between Baugh Fell and Abbotside Common; it continues along the length of Wensleydale before joining the River Swale near Boroughbridge to form the River Ouse.

At the next gate, just before Harker Beck, turn hard right away from the river along a path by woods. A gate leads onto the A6108. Taking care of passing traffic, turn left onto the road and continue for 400 yards. Go through the gate on your left and follow the path straight to the abbey.

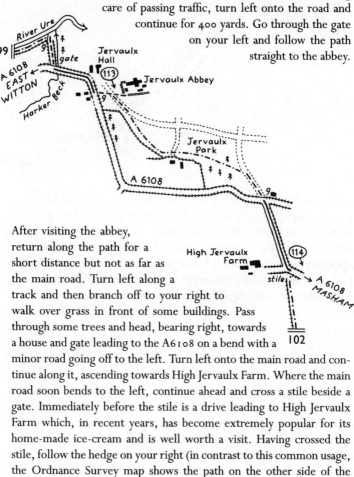

After visiting the abbey, return along the path for a short distance but not as far as the main road. Turn left along a track and then branch off to your right to walk over grass in front of some buildings. Pass through some trees and head, bearing right, towards a house and gate leading to the A6108 on a bend with a minor road going off to the left. Turn left onto the main road and continue along it, ascending towards High Jervaulx Farm. Where the main road soon bends to the left, continue ahead and cross a stile beside a gate. Immediately before the stile is a drive leading to High Jervaulx Farm which, in recent years, has become extremely popular for its home-made ice-cream and is well worth a visit. Having crossed the stile, follow the hedge on your right (in contrast to this common usage, the Ordnance Survey map shows the path on the other side of the hedge) through a field.

Jervaulx Abbey

This was a great Cistercian house, founded in 1156 and suppressed by Henry VIII in 1537. The abbey fell into ruins but there is still sufficient remaining to remind the walker of the way of life of the Cistercian monks who built and occupied it. Little remains of the church which is entered through the south-west door and was the focal point of the abbey. Other parts that can be seen include the cloister, the dining hall, two infirmaries and the abbot's lodging. The dominant feature is an imposing wall of the dormitory, originally 180 feet long with a line of lancet windows. The abbey is set in lovely parkland with many trees and flowers, the daffodils and aubrietia being particularly attractive in spring. The site is privately owned but is open daily all year and there is an admission charge.

Go through a gate and take another gate on your right and ascend heading for the brow of the hill. A stile leads to another field, then continue to ascend in the same direction going through a gap in a hedge to another field. Go through a gate and almost immediately through another gate leading to an enclosed track which is followed south into Ellingstring. Turn left onto a lane and the youth hostel is found on the right after a short distance.

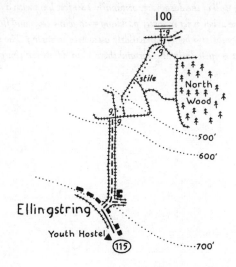

Ellingstring Youth Hostel to Thirsk

Distance: 21 miles (22 miles including deviation to Masham)
Going: Easy
Highest point: Ellingstring Youth Hostel – 722 feet
Map required: O. S. Pathfinder 630 Middleham & Jervaulx, 631 Bedale
  & Pickhill, 641 Ripon and 621 Thirsk

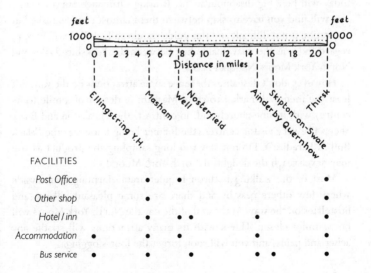

I must ask for your patience on today's walk as I have spent much time, energy and effort trying to find a satisfactory route across the Vale of York to Thirsk, a route which does involve too much road walking but many of my efforts have been thwarted.

My aim was to combine safe crossing-places of the A1, the River Swale and the main east coast railway line with good footpaths, but the options are few. Although all my crossings have bridges to make the walk as safe as possible, inevitably this has added to the 'tarmac' mileage. It is possible that a bridleway bridge may be built over the A1 near Middleton Quernhow which would reduce the amount of road walking; however, due to the usual financial constraints, it may be some way off yet. In the meantime, take advantage of the many grass verges along the lanes. I found trainers eased the foot pounding.

To those who like the high ridges and passes, open fells, heather moorlands, delightful riverside walking and undulating countryside, today will be a big disappointment. If using Ordnance Survey maps, you will find you have to skip between them almost continuously, but navigation is not difficult and this guide should suffice. You will have to regard today as the unavoidable link between the Yorkshire Dales and North York Moors National Parks.

However, don't despair as there are some attractions on the way, not least the medieval market town of Masham (a detour of a mile to its centre) with its fine church and, in contrast, the Theakston and Black Sheep Brewery visitor centres (the former being known as the 'Black Bull in Paradise'). Do not stay too long sampling the product as you may never reach the delightful North York Moors!

Most of the walking is through quiet arable farming countryside where few others pass by and there are some pleasant villages and hostelries on the way. At the end of the day the North York Moors will be 21 miles closer, Thirsk with its many attractions will soothe any aches and pains, and you will soon forget the foot-slogging.

From the youth hostel retrace the previous day's route along the road and turn right down the lane to where two tracks fork. Take the enclosed track on the right and where it comes to two gates go through the left one. Keep to the edge of fields in more or less a straight line, going through two gates. When another two gates side by side are reached, take the left-hand one. The path bears right and descends to a gate which leads to a grassy track. Go through two more gates.

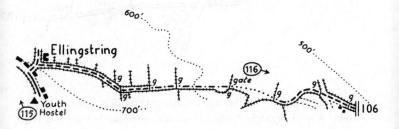

Enter High Ellington village; keep straight ahead past the tiny chapel built in 1877. This quiet lane shortly meets the A6108 Leyburn–Masham road. Cross over the road through a gate opening into a large field. Follow the fence/hedge on your right to a gate. Keep straight ahead, going through two more gates.

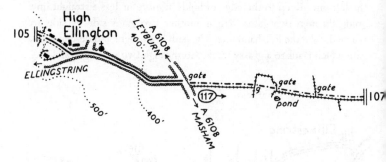

[*See* map opposite.] Go through another gate passing a quarry on your right. A track is reached which descends and bends left towards High Mains Farm, passing High Mains Cottages on your right. Go through two gates into a yard of High Mains Farm and leave by two gates on your right. The River Ure comes into sight on your left but loop round to the right and descend, over a stile towards the river. Head slightly away from the river to a stile at the right-hand side of a small wood. Carry on along the top edge of the wood, past a barn. Cross over a stile and through a gate, now leaving the wood behind. Go past Low Mains Farm and at another wood go over a stile, across the next field to a stile which leads over a small footbridge. Continue to follow the River Ure to a gate and stile and take the stile on the left over another footbridge which is gated on the far side. Continue to another stile and footbridge, and finally cross a stile leading onto the A6108. Those wishing to visit Masham should turn right onto the main road, the centre being approximately ½ mile further on [*see* page 108].

Those wishing to continue without stop should turn left over Masham Bridge. The present bridge was built in 1755 to replace the 200-year-old wooden bridge, washed away by flood in 1732. After crossing the bridge, go through a gate opposite into a large field and head for its far right-hand corner. Go over a stile which leads back onto the A6108.

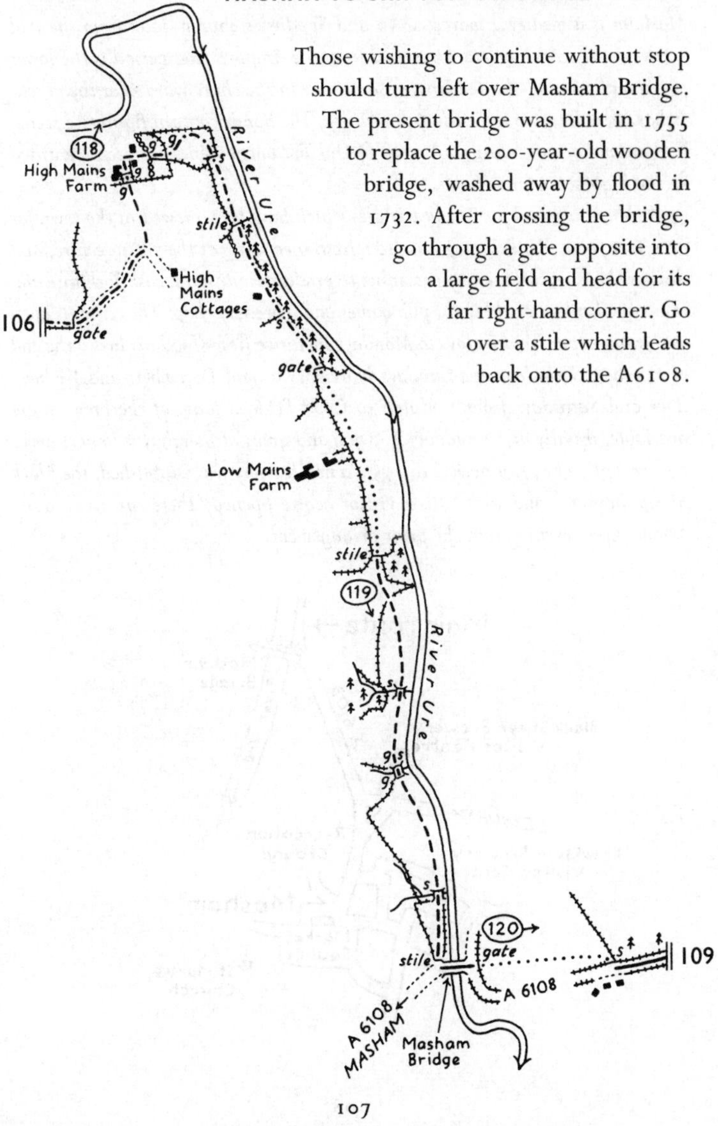

High Mains Farm

stile

High Mains Cottages

106 | gate

gate

Low Mains Farm

stile

119

Low Mains Farm

River Ure

120

gate

stile

A 6108

109

A 6108 MASHAM

Masham Bridge

118

River Ure

Deviation to Masham

Masham is a medieval market town and St Mary's church dates from the mid 12th century. An important survival from the Anglo-Saxon period is the lower portion of a round-shafted cross of sandstone in the churchyard near the porch. It has been dated to the early 9th century. The bands contain figurative scenes and animal ornamentation. A series of Old Testament scenes has been identified in the highest complete band.

Masham is noted for Theakston ales which have been brewed in the town for over 165 years. Walkers may want to refresh themselves at the visitor centre, and discover how a small brewery continues to produce traditional cask Yorkshire ale; there are displays of old tools, pub games and a brewery shop. The centre is open 10.30am–4pm, Wednesdays to Mondays inclusive from Good Friday to the end of October; Saturdays and Sundays November to mid-December; and Wednesdays and Saturdays from 1 March to Good Friday. Tours of the brewery are available, usually at 12 midday, 2.30pm and 4pm, although it is important to reserve a place by prior notice. In 1992 a new brewery was established, the Black Sheep Brewery, and in 1996 a visitor centre opened; there are tours daily 10am–5pm; evening tours by prior arrangement.

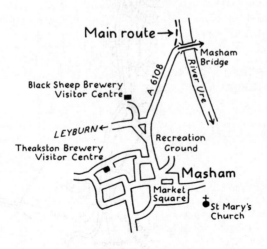

The main road is followed for 350 yards, but leave it by going straight on where it meets the B6267. In just over ½ mile, ignore the B6268 which goes off to your left. However, take the next lane on your left signposted to the village of Well.

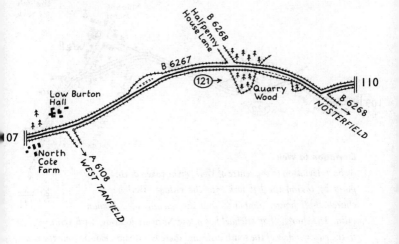

Continue along the lane (marked Masham Lane on the O. S. map) for about a mile until a fork is reached.

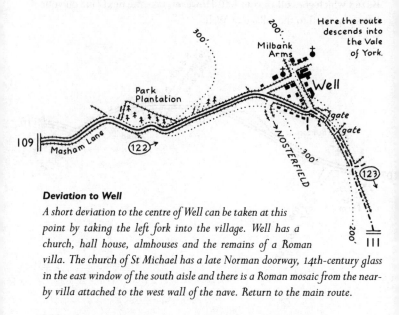

Deviation to Well

A short deviation to the centre of Well can be taken at this point by taking the left fork into the village. Well has a church, hall house, almshouses and the remains of a Roman villa. The church of St Michael has a late Norman doorway, 14th-century glass in the east window of the south aisle and there is a Roman mosaic from the near-by villa attached to the west wall of the nave. Return to the main route.

If not visiting Well, take the right-hand lane at the fork which ascends steeply to join another lane coming in from the right. Keep straight ahead to descend sharply to a bend in the lane just after a footpath sign on the right, which is ignored. Another footpath sign points to a short lane which is followed to a gate. Go through this and, shortly afterwards, another and follow the track to where a footpath branches off to the right of a hedge. Follow this path with the hedge on your left.

Continue to a gate which was in some disrepair when I last passed through it. Enter a very large field, past a plantation on your left and, leaving a fence on your right, proceed in a south-easterly direction. Pass through another plantation and cross a stile leading into a small field. Bear right to another stile and go to the right of farm buildings. Keeping in the same direction, go over two more stiles to join the B6267 opposite the Freemasons Arms, in Nosterfield village. Turn left along the road and almost immediately turn right down a lane. At a crossroads beyond the village carry straight on along a track for 700 yards and, at a T-junction, turn left onto a narrow lane. Note the henge on your left; not quite Stonehenge but nevertheless of some interest. The circles are three henge monuments thought to be of the early Bronze Age period. Follow the lane to Thornborough and bear right at a fork.

Follow the lane to a T-junction with another lane. Turn right here and after ½ mile a bridleway crosses the lane. Take the definite track on your left and follow this for ½ mile, going through two gates to reach the B6267. Turn right along the B-road and ignore all roads off to the left and right.

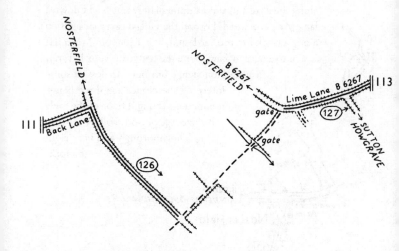

Taking care of passing traffic, follow the lane for just under two miles, keeping in mind that with every step on tarmac the North York Moors are drawing closer.

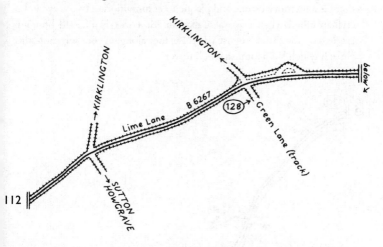

Continue until you go under the A1 and then continue on along the B6267 for a mile to go through Ainderby Quernhow.

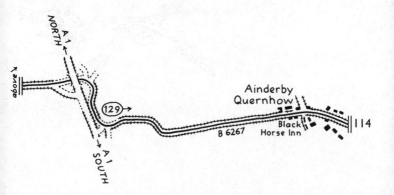

Follow the road to a T-junction reached in just over another mile. Turn left at the junction onto the busy A61 and walk over Skipton Bridge into Skipton-on-Swale. On your right, in front of Skipton Hall, there is a memorial stone and plaque to commemorate two crew and a civilian killed when a Royal Canadian Air Force Halifax III bomber crashed on the site in August 1944. Further along on your left, note the church which has an unusual bell tower.

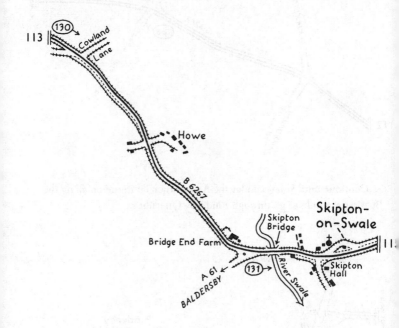

Continue to walk along the A61 using the grass verge on your right. Shortly after two small huts on your right, take a signposted bridle-way on the right. Keep straight ahead, ignoring tracks to the left and

right, until the hedge is reached and, by turning sharp left, follow the hedge to the main road (A167). Taking care of passing traffic, turn left at the road and soon after take a path on your right. This shortly joins a track which is followed to the left for ½ mile.

At the end of the track, go through a gate and back onto the A61. There is nothing for it but to turn right and follow the main road for approximately 2½ miles to Thirsk [see map page 116].

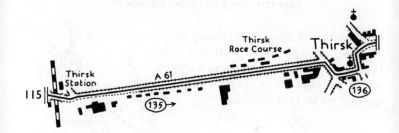

Thirsk

Thirsk is a market town and the route passes one of the most popular racecourses in the north. The grandstand was opened in 1854 and it hosts eight to ten flat race meetings each year.

In the Market Place is what is known as the Bull Ring, which is marked out in cobbles. This is where bulls were baited by dogs before going to slaughter, a nasty sport which took place as late as 1750. The buses now stand there. The Three Tuns was a bustling coaching inn with extensive stabling at the rear, some of which remains. The stagecoach trade provided employment for large numbers of townsfolk until the coming of the railway. Pevsner reckoned that St Mary's church, built in the Perpendicular style in the 15th century, is without question the most spectacular perpendicular church in North Yorkshire, so it is well worth a visit. The real James Herriot practiced in Thirsk and, at the time of writing, plans are afoot for the building to become a museum; the practice has moved to more peaceful surroundings elsewhere.

Thirsk to Helmsley Youth Hostel

Distance: 19 miles (20 miles including the detour to Rievaulx Abbey)
Going: Moderate to strenuous
Highest point: Hambleton Down – 1,017 feet
Map required: O. S. Pathfinder 621 Thirsk and O.S. Outdoor Leisure
   26 North York Moors, Western area

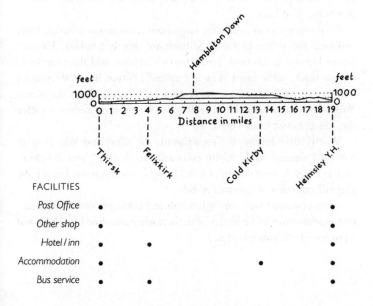

Today the North York Moors are reached of which St. Aelred, the 12th-century abbot of Rievaulx Abbey, wrote: 'Everywhere peace, everywhere serenity and a marvellous freedom from the tumult of the world.' This is still the case as we hurtle towards the millennium and it is re-assuring that considerable efforts are being made to preserve the National Parks.

We soon leave the flat Vale of York with its strips of tarmac and start to ascend along paths and tracks to the pleasant village of Felixkirk, nestling below the Hambleton Hills. After a steep ascent, the Cleveland Way is joined and followed, in reverse to its usual direction. Any Cleveland Way walkers you meet will be on the first day of their walk having started at Helmsley earlier in the day. Their walk, at 108 miles, is approximately half the distance of this and takes a wide northerly sweep through the North York Moors, eventually finishing south of Scarborough at Filey.

Continuing on our route, the magnificent viewpoints at Sutton Bank and near the White Horse of Kilburn are shortly reached. The late James Herriot in his book *James Herriot's Yorkshire* said the view from Sutton Bank 'is the finest view in England'. Sutton Bank information centre is worth a visit since it provides information about the North York Moors, and has a café providing much needed refreshments after the 700-ft ascent from Thirsk.

Shortly after leaving the escarpment, the Cleveland Way is again followed through Cold Kirby eventually to descend into delightful Nettle Dale. A short detour (a mile) is highly recommended to see the magnificent ruins of Rievaulx Abbey.

After a pleasant walk through woods and fields you enter the attractive market town of Helmsley with its castle ruins, fine hostelries and a purpose-built youth hostel.

From the centre of Thirsk, continue east, passing the Three Tuns Hotel on your right. Cross over Cod Beck at New Bridge and carry straight on at a roundabout. Follow the A170 signposted for Sutton Bank and Helmsley. The road starts to ascend to a bridge over the busy A19. Before the road starts to descend, take the signposted footpath on your left by walking down steps to a lane. The lane runs parallel with the A19 before a stile is crossed on your right. Follow the edge of the field to go over another stile into another field. Bear slightly left away from the hedge to a gap leading to a track which is followed ahead.

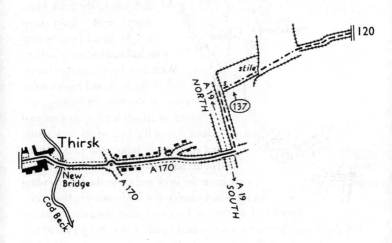

Continue along the track to Grizzle Field House, then bear to the left to go between the farmhouse and a large

Bellmoor Plantation

139

121

gate gate

Black Plantation

gate

FELIXKIRK

Whitelass Beck

stile

Grizzle Field House

138

119

gate

barn. Keep straight ahead over a fence (at the time of writing not gated or stiled) and, where the track bears sharp right, again keep straight ahead by a broken gate and head across a field to Whitelass Beck amongst trees. Follow the beck and cross a fence (also, at the time of writing, not gated or stiled) leading to a narrow lane. Cross the lane to go over a stile and continue to follow the beck. At the end of the field cross another stile. Bear right away from the beck and cross the field heading for a gap in the hedge that leads onto a narrow lane.

Turn left along the lane for a very short distance, then turn left along a track which soon becomes a path. Keep straight ahead to a gate to the right of Black Plantation. Bear right to cross through a line of trees. Cross over a small beck to go through a gap in the fence ahead. Follow the fence on your left to the end of the field and, after passing through a gate ahead, continue along a track. At a T-junction with another track turn right. Where the track turns left, keep straight ahead following a hedge on your left to cross a stile. Bear right to cross a bridge over a small beck. Continue to the corner of the field and go through the gate on your left. Follow the hedge on your right.

Continue ahead until a gate is reached. Turn right along a track which leads to a lane. Turn left to follow the lane past the Carpenter's Arms and enter the picturesque village of Felixkirk. Follow the road through the village, passing the Norman church of St Felix on your left. It is good to be leaving the flat Vale of York and to be walking uphill again.

FELIXKIRK TO SUTTON BANK

Where the lane forks, take the right branch for Boltby which ascends steeply away from the village, giving pleasant views to the village of Upsall on the left and the surrounding hills. A lodge is passed on your right and then at the second gate on your right turn onto a well-defined tarmac track. Follow this for ½ mile.

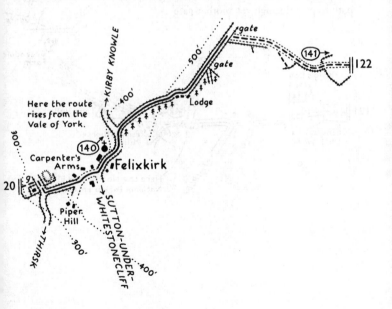

Go through a gate and pass by Cinque Cliff Wood; ignore all other tracks and paths. After going straight ahead for ⅔ mile, pass through two gates to reach a bend in a lane. Continue ahead along the lane and where it bends sharply left keep straight ahead on a track, at which point you enter the North York Moors National Park and a heavily gated section of the walk. The track crosses a ford with a footbridge alongside and then goes through a gate to pass Ravensthorpe Mill. The track ascends sharply and after another gate Tang Hall Farm is reached. Keep straight ahead and after a further gate bear left on another track and follow this to a gate leading near Greendale Farm. Pass to the left of the farm, going through two gates before the path bends left to a third gate to ascend towards Little Moor. A narrow path is followed until a gate is reached. After passing through the gate turn sharp right, continuing to ascend along the path to pass through yet another gate.

King's Bog Wood

BOLTBY →

121

Cinque Cliff Wood

142

gate

Ravensthorpe Mill

Tang Hall

Greendale Farm

THIRLBY

Here the North York Moors National Park is entered.

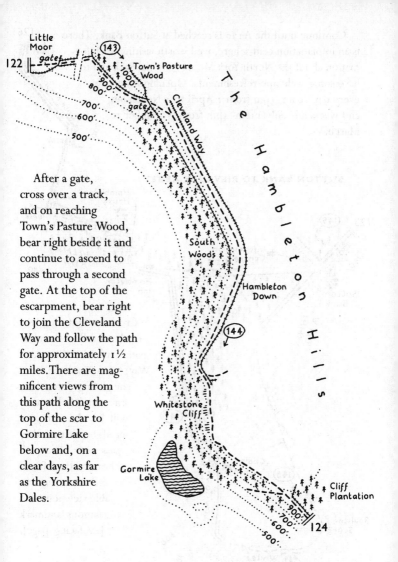

Little
Moor
gate
122

143
Town's Pasture
Wood

1000'
900'
800'
700'
600'
500'

gate

Cleveland Way

The Hambleton Hills

After a gate,
cross over a track,
and on reaching
Town's Pasture Wood,
bear right beside it and
continue to ascend to
pass through a second
gate. At the top of the
escarpment, bear right
to join the Cleveland
Way and follow the path
for approximately 1½
miles. There are mag-
nificent views from
this path along the
top of the scar to
Gormire Lake
below and, on a
clear days, as far
as the Yorkshire
Dales.

South
Woods

Hambleton
Down

144

Whitestone
Cliff

Gormire
Lake

Cliff
Plantation

900'
600'
500'

124

Continue until the A170 is reached at Sutton Bank. There is an information centre here, well worth visiting for information about the North York Moors National Park and to have some welcome refreshments. Opening times are every day 10am–5pm from 1 April to 1 November, and weekends only 11am–4pm from November to March.

SUTTON BANK TO RIEVAULX ABBEY

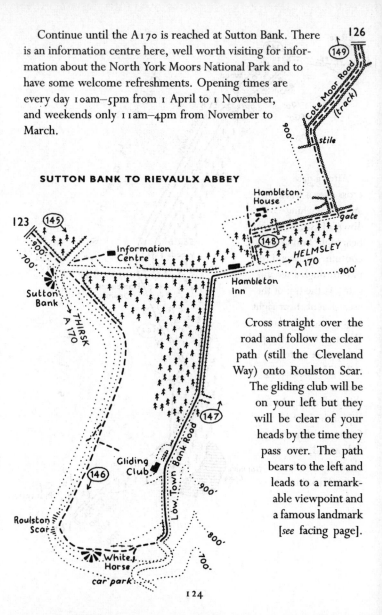

Cross straight over the road and follow the clear path (still the Cleveland Way) onto Roulston Scar. The gliding club will be on your left but they will be clear of your heads by the time they pass over. The path bears to the left and leads to a remarkable viewpoint and a famous landmark [see facing page].

The White Horse of Kilburn

The horse was carved out of the hillside in 1857 by John Hodgson, the village schoolmaster, with some thirty helpers. It is 314ft x 228ft. The underlying rock of the White Horse of Uffington in the south of England is chalk, but here it is limestone and the horse requires regular maintenance to keep its white coat.

It is not surprising that the plateau was the scene of large bonfires in 1977 to celebrate the Silver Jubilee of the Queen's accession to the throne, in 1988 to celebrate the 400th anniversary of the defeat of the Spanish Armada and in 1995 for the 40th anniversary of VE Day.

It was near here that the Battle of Byland was fought in 1322 when Edward II, whilst resting after an abortive raid into Scotland, was overtaken by the pursuing Scots. The English forces were defending the top of the escarpment but were eventually outflanked and had to retreat to York.

There is a splendid view to the south and on a clear day York Minster can be seen.

[*See* map opposite.] Carry on past the White Horse to leave the Cleveland Way, maintaining height and ignoring paths that descend off to your right. On reaching a lane, turn left and follow it past the gliding club now on your left, continuing until the A170 is reached at a T-junction. From here to Helmsley the Cleveland Way path is again followed; it is well defined and well signposted. At the A170, turn right to walk past the Hambleton Inn. Then, almost immediately, turn left down a track leading to Hambleton House. As the house comes into view, turn right along a narrow path which, after a stile, becomes a forest track. Before a gate turn left and follow the path to cross a stile. A track is then followed which bears right then left.

At a T-junction with a lane, turn right into the quiet village of Cold Kirby. Where the road forks, take a descending path in the middle of the fork, passing the church on your right. The path bends right and then ascends sharp left until a track is met called Low Field Lane. Keep straight ahead until a gate is reached, passing the three-quarter mark of the walk on the way. Then bear slightly right to go down a path alongside a fence/hedge at the field edge. A gate is soon reached leading into Callister Wood. The path joins a track after about 200 yards, at which point you turn left.

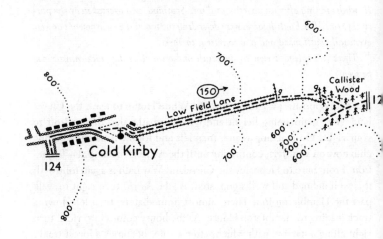

Follow the track which bends right until a gate is reached. Soon after the gate, go over a small footbridge. The stream crossed can be traced back to a spring at the base of a tree. Join another forestry track which passes some ponds on your left and skirts Noodle Hill on your right. On reaching a lane, just after a gate, turn left and follow the lane past the junction to Old Byland.

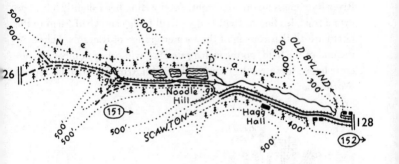

This lane shortly crosses the bridge over the River Rye and, at this point, a detour of a mile to the magnificent Rievaulx Abbey is strongly recommended (*see* facing page).

RIEVAULX ABBEY TO HELMSLEY

The main route follows the lane over a disused canal and then ascends steeply as the lane bends left. A path soon appears on your right leading to Quarry Bank Wood. Ascend the steep path, crossing over a stile, and continue ahead as a fine view down into the wooded valley of the River Rye opens up on your right. After a stile, head slightly left to go over a track leading to Griff Lodge; Griff Lodge and Griff Farm to the north are all that remain of the former grange of Rievaulx Abbey. At the end of the field, go through a gate. You will pass a number of concrete bases; these are the remains of a Polish Army camp of the Second World War.

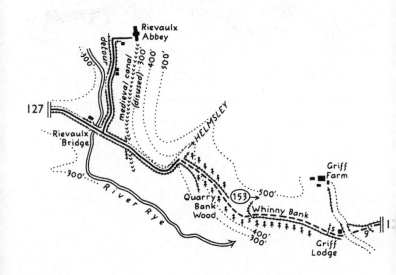

Detour to Rievaulx Abbey [*see* map opposite]

Turn left along a narrow lane and follow it for ½ mile until the entrance to Rievaulx Abbey is reached on your right.

The Cistercian abbey was founded by Walter l'Espec in 1132. Its importance can be judged by the fact that thirty-five years after it was founded there were 140 monks, 249 lay brothers and 260 hired laymen, a large community. The Abbey nestles in a tree-covered valley whose narrowness accounts for the fact that the church is aligned from north to south instead of from the usual east to west. The monks created great wealth from sheep farming (at one time they owned 14,000 sheep), iron working, fishing and salt production on the coast. Canals were used for floating blocks of stone on rafts from the River Rye to the Abbey for carving. Around the time of the Dissolution, however, the abbey declined and fell into debt and by 1536 only twenty-two monks remained. After 400 years of life, the site was eventually stripped for building stone and, in due course, passed to the Duncombe family. It was acquired by the state in 1918, and is now superbly looked after by English Heritage. The Abbey is open daily 10am–6pm from 1 April to 30 September, and daily 10am–4pm from 1 October to 31 March. There is an admission charge.

From the abbey, retrace your steps back to rejoin the lane by Rievaulx Bridge.

Descend into a wooded valley, cross a track in the bottom and then climb out the other side. Pass through a gate and shortly cross over a stile. Turn left at the end of the field and follow the field edge to a stile on your right. Follow the farm lane, going over two stiles, until a car park is reached, at which point Helmsley Castle can be seen on your right. This is in fact the start of the Cleveland Way, and a stone sculpture marks the spot. To reach the youth hostel turn right onto the B1257 and then left after the Feversham Arms Hotel to walk past the church. Follow the road round to the left and at a junction turn right and the hostel is on your right just before a T- junction.

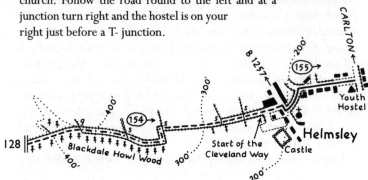

Helmsley

Helmsley lies under the southern edge of the North York Moors and is a typical small market town with a large market place surrounded by old inns and interesting shops.

The ruined castle stands high on a mound overlooking the town. It was built in about 1200 and was later besieged by Parliamentary forces after the battle of Marston Moor and the fall of York during the Civil War. The castle was finally surrendered on 22 November 1644 after a three-month siege. Between 1646 and 1647 the castle was made unfit for war with parts of the keep and the walls being destroyed. It is now in the hands of English Heritage and is open daily 10am–6pm from 1 April to 30 September, daily 10am–4pm from 1 October to 31 October and on Wednesday to Sunday 10am–4pm from 1 November to 31 March.

Helmsley Youth Hostel to Hutton-le-Hole

Distance: 13½ miles
Going: Moderate
Highest point: Rollgate Bank – 971 feet
Map required: O. S. Outdoor Leisure 26 North York Moors,
   Western area

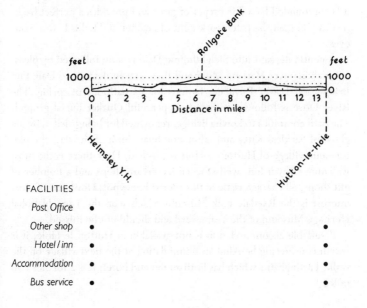

FACILITIES

	Helmsley Y.H.	Hutton-le-Hole
Post Office	•	
Other shop	•	•
Hotel / inn	•	•
Accommodation	•	•
Bus service	•	•

Today's walk is relatively short but you are recommended to stock up with provisions before you start as there is no opportunity to obtain proper provisions until your arrival at Scalby, near Scarborough, on the last day. You will see few other walkers until you arrive at Farndale, towards the end of this day's walk. There is some very good valley and moorland walking, as you cross from one valley to another, and in fine weather there are some delightful picnic spots on the way.

After a gentle ascent out of Helmsley the secluded Riccal Dale is followed north and then crossed until a steady climb along a straight lane leads up to Rollgate Bank. Here I would like to recommend an ideal lunchtime stop – at my adopted O. S. column, where there are some of the finest views of moorland on the North York Moors, towards Sleightholme Dale and Bransdale; it is well worth stopping here for awhile to savour the peace and fine open views. Unlike many trig points it is surrounded by a fine carpet of grass and provides a perfect backrest as you scan the patchwork quilt of heather and fields before your eyes.

A gentle descent into Sleightholme Dale is soon followed by pleasant walking over Harland Moor and then a steep descent to Dale End Bridge and Lower Farndale, famous for its daffodils in spring. The River Dove is followed to pass by a peaceful Quaker burial ground. The path continues to Lowna Bridge, renowned for being visited by the ghost of Sarkless Kitty and, after one final climb of the day, the picturesque village of Hutton-le-Hole is reached. Here there is the most welcome Crown Inn, well-stocked ice-cream shops and a number of gift shops; all characteristic of this tourist honeypot. However, of most interest is the Ryedale Folk Museum which won the 1995 National Heritage Museum of the Year award and should not be missed.

If suitable accommodation is not available in Hutton-le-Hole, it is worth considering booking accommodation at the next village on the walk, Lastingham, which has both an inn and hotel; it is a further two miles.

From the youth hostel turn right along the lane and almost immediately take the track (signposted public footpath) on your left which leads along the back of some stone-built bungalows on your left. Some older Ordnance Survey maps incorrectly show a right of way on the other side of the bungalows. Go through a gate to enter a field, initially following the hedge on your right and then bearing left to a gate in the left corner of the field. The following section is heavily gated. Continue to bear left as the path ascends to go through two gates. There are fine retrospective views to Helmsley, and the castle tower in particular can be picked out above the red tile roofs of modern buildings. After the second gate, follow the hedge on your right and ascend to a gate below Monk Holme Wood. Go through the next gate and ascend steeply to a gate near Reagarth Farm. Shortly go through another gate and cross Monk Gardens Lane to yet another. Walk along the field edge to the top of the field and then descend to a gate leading into Riccal Dale Wood. After the gate immediately turn left to follow the fence on your left.

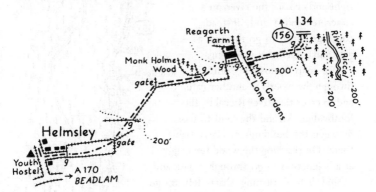

Do not descend on any paths to the bottom of the valley and instead follow the wood's fence on your left. Rea Garth Farm soon comes into view and after two gates the track passes between buildings. Leave the farm by another gate. The clear track continues along the edge of the woods to pass through three gates. After the third gate, at a fork, take the descending track off to your right; you will enjoy walking through this quiet, peaceful, wooded valley. Another track joins from the right but continue in the same direction. Then at a fork of tracks, take the right-hand branch that descends to the valley bottom. Ignore the track that goes off to your right and crosses the river on a concrete bridge and, instead, continue ahead to go through a gate and soon enter a clearing.

[*See* map opposite] Continue through the woods to another gate and to cross the River Riccal by the footbridge. Ascend the field to pass between the buildings of Hasty Bank Farm. On reaching the wood turn right at a T-junction to go through a gate and ascend before turning sharp left to go through another gate. Veer right along a track across the field and go through another gate to reach a lane from Pockley to Birk Nab Farm. Here the walk teeters on the edge of the

National Park boundary but does not leave it. Cross the road and go through a gate to follow the field edge until a gate appears on your right which you go through. Descend into a wooded valley, going through a second gate, and then climb up on the other side to go through a third gate. Keeping the hedge on your right proceed to a gate which leads onto a lane. Turn left and walk up the lane past Middle Farm and High Farm. After a gate, the lane becomes track and, looking back, there are good views to Ryedale. Another gate leads to a strip of conifer wood and then the track ascends open moorland to go through another gate near my adopted O. S. column. Descend Rollgate Bank on the steep track and at the bottom swing sharp right to skirt marshy ground forming Great Runnell. Bear left, following the fence on your left for a short distance.

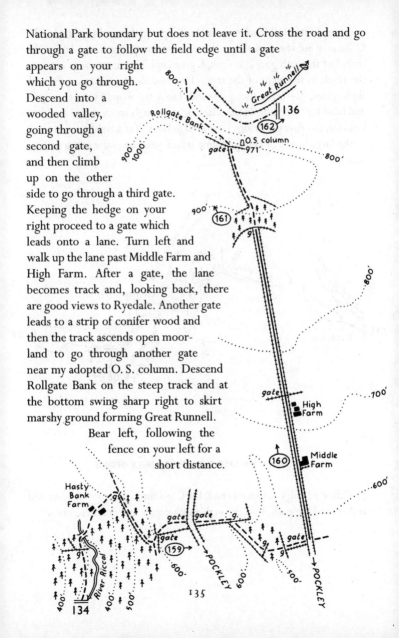

Ascend Otterhill Common and bear right to descend to a track. The Ordnance Survey map shows the right of way going to the left of the trees but the path goes onto rough grassland. Common usage is to use the track to the right of the trees. Descend the track to pass through three gates, the last entering a wood. Leave the wood by another gate, and head for Otterhills Farm. Turn right through another gate and then bear left to cross the bridge over Hodge Beck. Turn right along a track to the large house of Penny Holme which you pass; now join a narrow lane.

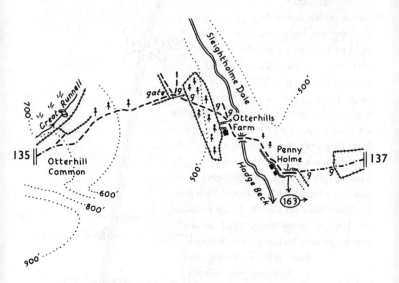

PENNY HOLME TO HUTTON-LE-HOLE

Just after a bridge crosses a small beck, go through a gate on your left and ascend the path. Pass through another gate and continue ahead.

Cross a stile and continue to ascend with a hedge and then wall on your right. When a hedge swings away to the right, continue to a gate which gives access to a track through Stonely Woods. After Stonely Woods House, turn left along the access lane and, when the lane turns right, ascend the track ahead. The path passes a former school on your right and then bears right. It then bears left through a gate and along a grassy track on the edge of the woods. Turn left near Common House and then right

onto a broad track leading to a lane at Hope Inn Farm. Turn left along the lane and after a right- and left-hand bend, take the gate on your right. Follow the wall and hedge on your right for a short distance and then bear to the left on a path over rough moorland. Go through a gate and then over a small bridge over a ditch. Continue to a gap in a stone wall and follow a track down the hillside to cross the Harland Beck over a footbridge. Go through a gate into a field and then turn right to go through another gate.

The track swings left and, ignoring a path off to your left, continues through heather to a lane near a cairn. Cross the lane and descend a path to a track. Turn right and cross a stile on your left. There are fine

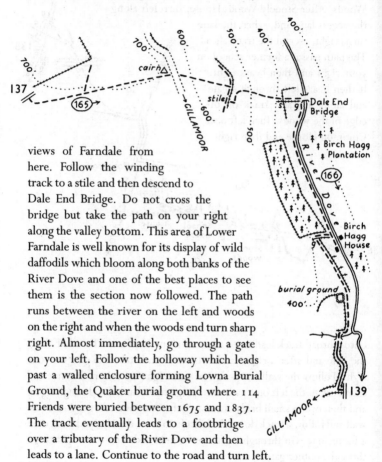

views of Farndale from here. Follow the winding track to a stile and then descend to Dale End Bridge. Do not cross the bridge but take the path on your right along the valley bottom. This area of Lower Farndale is well known for its display of wild daffodils which bloom along both banks of the River Dove and one of the best places to see them is the section now followed. The path runs between the river on the left and woods on the right and when the woods end turn sharp right. Almost immediately, go through a gate on your left. Follow the holloway which leads past a walled enclosure forming Lowna Burial Ground, the Quaker burial ground where 114 Friends were buried between 1675 and 1837. The track eventually leads to a footbridge over a tributary of the River Dove and then leads to a lane. Continue to the road and turn left.

Continue along the road which crosses Lowna Bridge. The building on the left of the bridge used to be a tanning and bone-crushing mill; it was in use until about 1914. Continue along the moorland road for ¾ mile and, where it joins the road coming south from Blakey, turn right to descend into Hutton-le-Hole. At the fork, keep left to cross over the stream and pass the Crown Inn on your left.

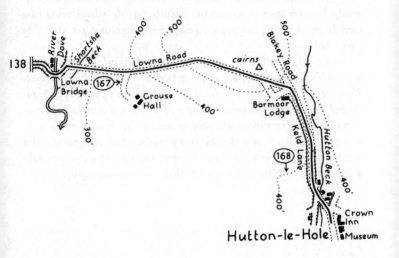

Hutton-le-Hole

Hutton-le-Hole appears as Hoton in the great Domesday survey of 1085–86, thereafter undergoing several name changes from Hege-Hoton, Hoton under Heg and Newton, to Hutton-in-the-Hole by the 17th century; the present form dates from only the 19th century.

Alongside the strong craft tradition in the area, in particular spinning and weaving, other industries such as tanning and milling, lime-burning and coal mining have left their marks and two centuries ago the village would have seemed a very different place from the quiet and well-manicured spot admired by visitors today.

The Ryedale Folk Museum, spread over 2½ acres of land, contains a reconstructed hamlet of workshops, thatched cottages and a thatched manor house. There are also barns, mills, a medieval glass kiln, an early photographer's studio and wagon sheds. The museum has a number of special craft demonstration days each year. The museum also runs an annual Merrills contest: this is an ancient, skilled board game that has been played regularly in the area and is now, in fact, increasing in popularity. It is open 10am–5.30pm (last admission 4.30pm) from 17 March to 27 October. There is an admission charge.

Hutton-le-Hole to Lockton Youth Hostel

Distance: 13½ miles

Going: Moderate

Highest point: High Muffles Farm – 885 feet

Map required: O. S. Outdoor Leisure 26 North York Moors, Western
area and 27 North York Moors, Eastern area

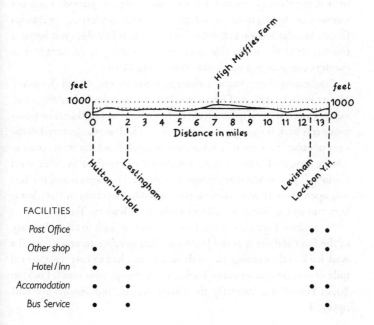

As with the previous day the mileage on this penultimate day is relatively low and, although there are no major ascents and descents, there are plenty of minor ones. There are few opportunities to obtain refreshments and you are recommended to carry what you need.

After leaving Hutton-le Hole a pleasant climb gives fine views of the surrounding moorland, including much of the previous day's walk, before you arrive at the picturesque and charming village of Lastingham. The church should be visited to see the fine crypt, unchanged since the 11th century. On leaving Lastingham there is an ascent onto open moorland which feels quite remote, especially in mist. Careful route-finding is needed on this section as some of the paths through heather are faint. After crossing the River Seven there are a few miles of walking through conifer forestry until Stape is passed. I am not enamoured by sections of softwoods, much preferring deciduous forest, but the section is not too long and therefore does not become tedious. It is inevitable that some forest walking is encountered as conifers cover large areas of the North York Moors.

Continuing from Stape a descent leads to the North Yorkshire Moors Railway station of Levisham (in fact, 1½ miles before the actual village) and a short trip on a train (often steam) to Goathland or Grosmont and back is strongly recommended. The line was featured in the very popular 'Heartbeat' television series and, from the train, you can admire much of what is now commonly referred to as 'Heartbeat Country'. The route was devised by George Stephenson and the line was opened on 26 May 1836. It was closed by Beeching in 1965 but is now run by the North York Moors Historical Railway Trust.

Levisham village is soon reached and you may wish to take advantage of the food and drink at the Horseshoe Inn in order to save yourself a walk back in the evening. If you think you have had an easy day the final mile of descent and ascent to Lockton will change your mind. Lockton Youth Hostel was formerly the village school, but lessons are now optional.

The route sets off south past the museum and church and just before a junction of roads take the path on the left alongside the beck, going over a stile. Keep the stream on the left. Ascend steeply to go through a gate, now heading away from the stream. Turn left and immediately cross a stile on your right. Follow the path over another stile and along an old holloway until it turns left. Then the path turns right to follow a stone wall on your left. There are good views north towards Spaunton Moor and Hutton Ridge, and further away to the north-west the TV transmitting mast on Bilsdale Moor can be seen. There are also views over the Vale of Pickering and the Tabular Hills to the south. At the end of the field, turn left and then right to follow a farm road. The road swings right and then bears left through the buildings of Grange Farm. After crossing a cattle grid, turn right at the road. Take the first left along the road leading to Spaunton village.

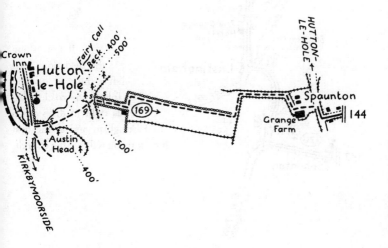

Deviation to Victoria Cross

Immediately before the next road junction a short deviation left along an ascending path (in common usage but not marked as a right of way on the Ordnance Survey map) to Victoria Cross can be taken. The cross was erected in 1897 to commemorate Queen Victoria's Jubilee and the opening of the road up Lidsty Hill on which the cross now stands. From the cross there is a superb view of Lastingham, nestling in the hollow, and the wide open Spaunton Moor. The path descends from the cross to rejoin the main route.

Tranmire Beck

Grain Beck

small cairn

Askew Rigg

500'

400'

500'

400'

171

Hole Beck

400'

The Grange Hotel

400'

Blacksmiths Arms Inn

400'

500'

Lastingham

Ings Beck

400'

500'

Victoria Cross

170

143

Spaunton

APPLETON-LE-MOORS

If not taking the deviation, turn left at the road junction to follow the road which bends right to drop down to Lastingham and at the first junction you will see the church.

Lastingham

Lastingham was chosen as a site for a monastery by St Cedd in 654 but it was destroyed by the Danes about two hundred years later. In 1078 some monks from Whitby re-founded the abbey but after ten years moved on to York where they founded St Mary's Abbey. The present church has a remarkable crypt which is probably still as it was nearly 1,000 years ago. It is reached down a stairway inside the church and is unique in England in having a nave and side aisles. It is believed to have been used at one time for cockfighting.

As you cross over Hole Beck, just beyond the road after the church, St Cedd's Well is passed. It is covered by a canopy of stone taken from Rosedale Priory. On a board is a Latin inscription reading: 'Cedd founder of Lastingham Monastery died AD664–5, buried on the right-hand side of the altar'.

LASTINGHAM TO STAPE

From the church, having passed the road to Hutton-le-Hole on your left, proceed to the next junction; turn left here and head north out of the village passing the Grange Country House Hotel on your right. Go through a gate which leads to a track. At a junction of tracks follow the right-hand track with a wall on your right. Leave the wall and go past an enclosure on your left and, bearing left, drop down to a small valley. Cross the stream, Tranmire Beck, and take the path which ascends the other side of the valley in a north-easterly direction. The path becomes very faint and, at times, indistinct. Near a small cairn it crosses a ridge track to descend through heather.

Descend ahead to a bridleway and turn left onto it to head north parallel with the River Seven. Do not try to cut a corner by following the path shown directly ahead on the Ordnance Survey map as there is no bridge where it reaches the river. After ¾ mile, at some enclosed fields, turn sharp right towards the river through a gate into a field and bear slightly left to leave the field on the other side by a gate: this differs from the right of way shown on the Ordnance Survey map beyond the enclosed fields, but our path is the accepted route through common usage. Turn right through the next field to reach the river which is crossed by a modern concrete and steel footbridge. [*cont. opposite*]

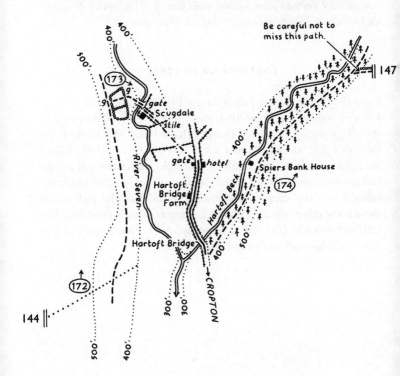

[*See* map opposite] Go through a gate and pass Scugdale Cottage on your right. Ascend the path to cross a stile into a field. Pass through a gap in the hedge and cross the next field, bearing right between large patches of gorse. Head for a gate and turn right onto the road opposite the hotel, the Blacksmiths Arms. Walk down the road to cross Hartoft Bridge and almost immediately afterwards turn left along a forestry road. Follow the forest road for nearly ½ mile keeping parallel with the valley bottom and passing Spiers Bank House on your left. About half a mile further on, be careful not to miss an important right turn. Where the track bears left, take a way-marked forest path to the right. After a few yards a broken-down stone wall is reached on your left; this was a former field boundary before the area was afforested. It will be a left-hand guide for the next few hundred yards.

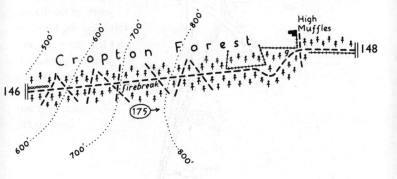

As you continue ahead a number of forestry roads cross your route. At a point where the path joins a firebreak, continue along the firebreak. This section is marked by yellow arrows. The firebreak joins a road which swings right and then left to pass a gate. Walk to the south of High Muffles Farm and continue to follow the forest road heading east with a fence on your right.

The road bears right and then left before reaching a junction of forest tracks. Head south-easterly by turning right for 150 yards along a track. At a junction of forest roads, continue ahead along a sunken track to pass the hamlet of Stape.

STAPE TO LOCKTON YOUTH HOSTEL

Where the track joins the lane from Stape continue along the lane for just over ¼ mile and opposite the buildings of Taylor Hill, take a track on the left. Go through a series of gates south of the forest, following the fence on your left. After six gates and a plantation, take the enclosed bridleway off to your right and head south.

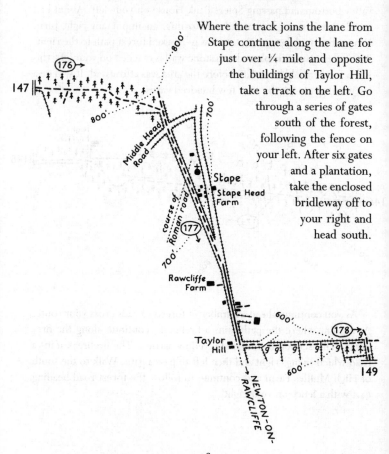

Shortly pass Middle Farm on your left. The right of way crosses Stony Moor and, after crossing a small beck, you bear left through a gate and then ascend right. If refreshments are needed, a short detour can be made to Newton-on-Rawcliffe, approximately 500 yards further along the track. Otherwise take a stile on your left and follow the path descending the valley side in a south-easterly direction. Go through a gate and continue to descend to a footbridge over a beck. Follow the track for 50 yards and cross over the railway line at Levisham station. At this point, with only 2½ miles to go before reaching Lockton, and you may wish to consider a brief trip on a train to Goathland or Grosmont if time allows.

Follow the road ascending steeply away from the station. Shortly after trees on your right, take a track which cuts the corner off the

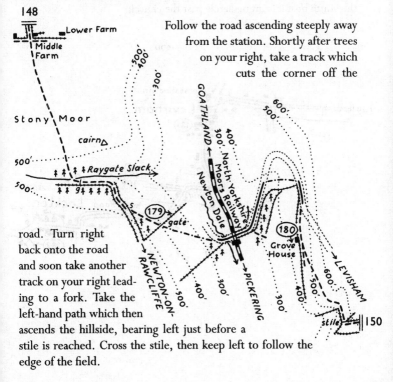

road. Turn right back onto the road and soon take another track on your right leading to a fork. Take the left-hand path which then ascends the hillside, bearing left just before a stile is reached. Cross the stile, then keep left to follow the edge of the field.

Cross a stile and continue to follow the field edge to another stile which leads into a lane which is followed ahead. The lane bends right until a road is reached near the Horseshoe Inn. Turn right and walk past the church on your right to enter Levisham village. The village's original church and mill stand in the bottom of the ravine on the way to Lockton, suggesting that the village may have moved to its present site some centuries ago. It now stands on a plateau with a broad green in the middle, and the inn and maypole at its head. Continue along the road right through the village and descend the steep ravine with Levisham Mill in the bottom. Follow the road to climb to the village of Lockton. At a crossroads, turn left to walk past the church on your left; the youth hostel is immediately past the church.

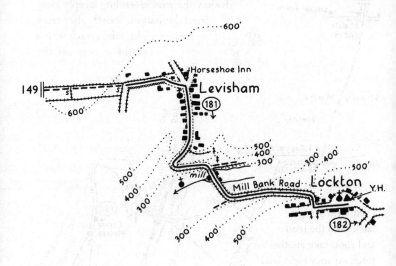

Lockton Youth Hostel to Scarborough

Distance: 18 (20¼ miles including the detour to the Bridestones
  Nature Reserve)
Going: Moderate
Highest point: Viewpoint top of Hole of Horcum – 915 feet
Map required: O. S. Outdoor Leisure 27 North York Moors,
  Eastern area

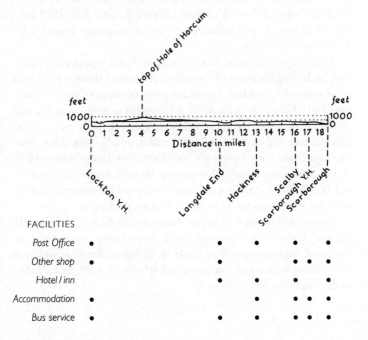

As with the first day of the walk, the last day is one to be savoured with some delightful countryside, stunning views, as well as places of interest along the way. Although you will wish to feel sea-breezes again and see the North Sea, do not rush the last day as there is much to see and enjoy. Refreshments are few and far between and you are advised to carry sufficient food and drink for the day. However, the hamlet of Langdale End has an inn which can provide welcome 'liquid' refreshment.

After leaving Lockton the route descends to the secluded Levisham Beck before following the valley north to reach the magnificent Hole of Horcum. There are dramatic retrospective views as you ascend out of the huge hollow. The curiously named Old Wife's Way is followed until the National Trust Bridestones Nature Reserve is reached and a detour is strongly recommended to see the unusually shaped Bride Stone rock formations.

Returning to the main route, Crosscliff Wood viewpoint is passed and, on leaving the forest, there is pleasant walking through fields with good views of Troutsdale. A walk along the 'forest drive' leads to Langdale End. After a steep ascent to a viewpoint near Broxa and a walk along Broxa Rigg, Hackness village is reached, with its attractive church, lake and hall in a delightful valley setting. Soon after, Scarborough Castle comes into view, the North York Moors National Park is left with regret and, after passing through Scalby, the coast is reached. Walkers staying at the youth hostel and finishing the walk the next day should make a short detour to it south along the A165.

You can give yourself a congratulatory 'pat on the back' as you make the final descent to Scarborough North Bay and, after 200 miles, journey's end. Scarborough offers plenty of 'fleshpots' for those who wish to celebrate in that way, but for me a Scarborough waffle and a paddle in the North Sea were sufficient!

Leave the youth hostel and turn left to follow the road. Shortly after a junction, where another road joins from the right, take a gate on your left. Follow the path which starts to descend into the valley. Go through a gate and go left at a fork of paths to descend to another gate. Follow the fence on your left and as it swings right, the path forks again, keep left to a gate and a footbridge over Levisham Beck. Ascend the other side of the valley, ignoring paths off to your left. Near the top of the valley, turn very sharply right (almost back on your tracks) and head east and then north, parallel with Levisham Beck until, after a gate, the path forks. Take the right-hand path and cross over two footbridges. With the beck now on your left, cross over a stile, and then go through a wall gap.

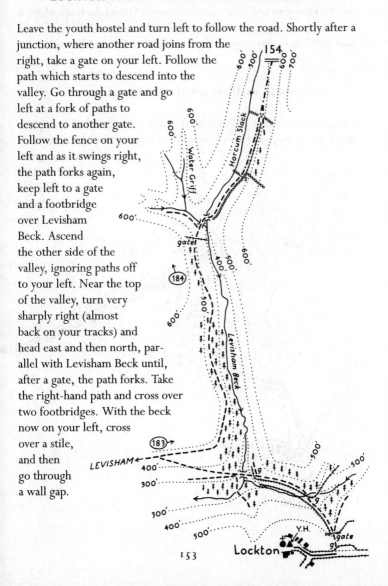

After a stile, pass Low Horcum farm on your right. Cross another stile beside a gate and cross over the stream. Ascend the track which is quite steep leading to a stile. Turn right at the stile and follow the main road as it bears right to give a fine view of the Hole and beyond.

HOLE OF HORCUM TO LANGDALE END

Cross over the road and just before the large car park and viewing point take a track on your left which leads to a gate. After the gate, keep straight ahead along the track called the Old Wife's Way for nearly a mile.

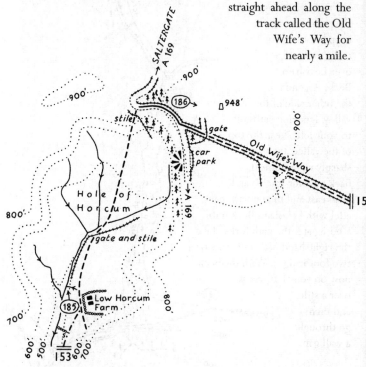

Hole of Horcum

The Hole is very dramatic and atmospheric and changes substantially in appearance and colour according to the time of day as well as the time of year. In winter, snow can accentuate the vastness of the hollow whilst in autumn, mist can make it grey and eerie. It is best viewed from near the car park at the top of the Hole, a place which can get quite busy with stopping motorists. Having walked 186 miles your appreciation of this wonderful scene will be much greater than theirs! From here, the moor falls away 400 feet into the huge hollow you have just walked through. According to legend, the hollow was created by a giant who scooped a handful of moor and threw it at his wife: he missed and the handful of moor formed Blakey Topping. However, the real reason for the formation of the hollow is that springs between the lower calcareous grit and the Oxford clay eroded away the hillside. The softer Oxford clay eroded more quickly and undermined the layers of rock which collapsed and enlarged the hollow to its present size. All the soil and clay from the valley has been washed down by the small stream.

Blakey Topping, at 875 feet, can be seen on your left and is thought to have had some religious significance during prehistoric times; it is now owned by the National Trust. Looking back and left, the Fylingdales early warning radar station can be seen, the former 'golf ball' structures having been replaced with the less attractive sand castle-shaped building. Cross over a lane which leads left to Newgate Foot. Keep to the top of Newgate Brow by going through a gate and heading

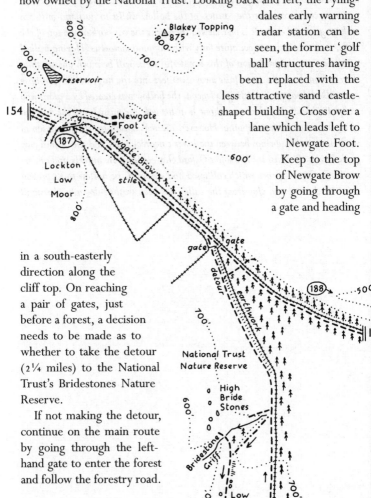

in a south-easterly direction along the cliff top. On reaching a pair of gates, just before a forest, a decision needs to be made as to whether to take the detour (2¼ miles) to the National Trust's Bridestones Nature Reserve.

If not making the detour, continue on the main route by going through the left-hand gate to enter the forest and follow the forestry road.

Detour to the National Trust's Bridestones Nature Reserve

Take the first gate, on your right, along a permissive track leading to the public right of way. The broad track descends gently to a dip at the head of Bridestone Griff which is a valley separating the High and Low Bride Stones. Do not take the first path on your right which is before the stream but instead take the second path on your right, just after the stream. The path ascends through heather to skirt some trees and then starts to descend gently to reach another path. Note the rock formations of the High Bride Stones on your right. Turn left to follow the path to the Low Bride Stones. These free-standing rocks of alternating layers of hard and softer Jurassic sandstone have been eroded and weathered by frost, wind and rain resulting in fantastic shapes, some of which seem to defy gravity. The Bridestones Nature Reserve extends over about 300 acres and contains many types of animals and plants typical of the North York Moors, but also some uncommon and rare species. When the last rock outcrop is reached, turn left to head east along a very clear path, ignoring the path straight ahead and other paths going off to your right. The path bends around to the left to head north, becoming a broad track again. Ascend the track to reach the head of Bridestone Griff once more, continue straight on to return to the main route, onto which you turn right.

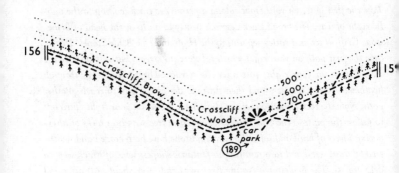

Continue along the cliff top, Crosscliff Brow, to Crosscliff Wood where there is a fine viewpoint towards (looking left to right) Blakey Topping, Fylingdales radar station, Thompson's Rigg, Allerston High Moor, Crosscliff Lake and the Langdale Forest. From the viewpoint, continue along the cliff edge in a north-easterly direction, ignoring a path on your left after approximately 700 yards.

After approximately a further 700 yards a small clearing on your left is reached. Here take the path on your left, faint at first, which descends the steep hillside. Where the path joins a track, turn left and then turn right at another track and after 100 yards a lane is joined. Turn right and climb towards Noddle Farm which you pass to the right. At a road junction turn right to pass a telephone kiosk on your left. Where the lane starts to bend right, cross a stile on your left and immediately turn right to cross over another stile. Turn left and follow the fence on your left, going over four stiles to pass to the south of Bickley Rigg Farm. (Older Ordnance Survey maps may show a different right of way as, prior to the present well-marked right of way, the path used to pass to the north of the farm.)

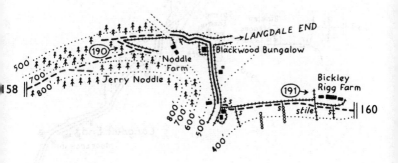

After passing the farm continue towards another two stiles and, after the second, turn sharp right to descend to cross another stile. Turn left to follow the hedge on your left, taking the opportunity to admire the fine views of Troutsdale in the south and to Wykeham Forest in the south-east. Pass Bickley Cottages on your left and, after crossing a stile and a footbridge, follow the wall on your left. After another stile, bear right and descend to a gate, and then bear left towards an oak tree immediately behind which a stile is crossed. Turn left along a track and, on joining a lane, turn right to cross a bridge over Black Beck. The lane is then followed to the hamlet of Langdale End where the Moorcock Inn might prove a diversion.

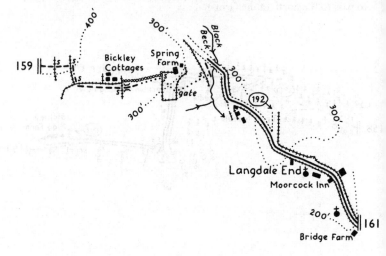

LANGDALE END TO HACKNESS

Leave the village, descending down the hill to pass the picturesque church of St Peter on your right.

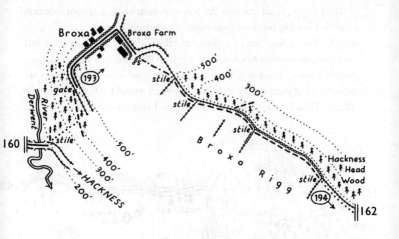

Cross the bridge over the River Derwent and immediately go over a stile on your left. Do not follow the river path but instead bear right to ascend the steep path which leads to a field. Head upwards to the left-hand corner of the field: the path is indistinct through the field but becomes clearer as it ascends steeply through bushes. When you reach a bridleway turn left and continue to ascend until a gate leads to a lane. Follow the lane left and upwards and, where it bends right, look over the wall on your left for a fine viewpoint. It is possible to see as far as Blakey Topping, which you passed six miles earlier. Continue along the lane to enter the small hamlet of Broxa. After passing a telephone kiosk and Broxa Farm on your right, turn right along a tarmacked track. At the end of the track cross a stile and head diagonally across the field to the left-hand corner. Cross over a stile and follow the path along Broxa Rigg, crossing three more stiles. There are fine views through the trees to High Dales and Whisper Dales running north, and Low Dales running south-east.

After a gate, head towards the fence on your right and continue until a gate is found in trees on your right. Go through the gate to follow the steeply descending track; a charcoal kiln will be passed on your left. On reaching another track follow it left to descend to a gate. Hackness church's spire, Hackness Hall and lake will be seen ahead. Turn left onto the road and, at a fork, follow the road round to the right into the village of Hackness, to pass the school and church on your right.

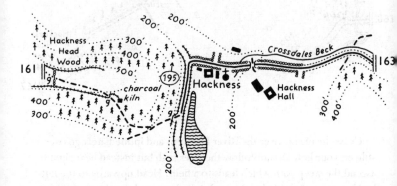

Hackness

The attractive church of St Peter is thought to be the oldest church in the Scarborough Deanery and is well worth a visit. Much of the church is 12th century, but the notable chancel arch is even earlier. There is an outstanding font, with a tall oak cover carved in 1480. Of especial interest are the carved stalls with misericords.

The impressive Hackness Hall, not open to the public, was built in 1791 by Carr of York. Its attractive gardens and parkland enhance the beautiful setting of the village.

HACKNESS TO SCALBY

Continue along the road passing the entrance to Hackness Hall.

Some 350 yards after a former lodge, where the road ascends steeply, take a footpath on your right. The path ascends through trees to a lane which is crossed to go through a gate on the opposite side. Follow the track ahead and, shortly after it becomes enclosed, turn right at a wall to go through a gate. Immediately turn left to follow the hedge on your left and then cross a wall by a ladder-stile. Keep straight ahead on a faint path to cross a stile next to a wood.

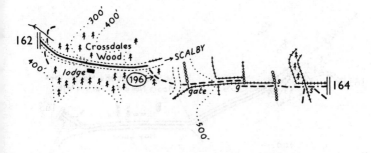

Follow a hedge on your left and soon there are fine views ahead with the North Sea being seen for the first time, some three miles away. At the end of the hedge the path descends through trees, along a holloway, to a stile. After crossing the stile, follow the clear path as it descends and leave the woods by another stile. From this field, Scarborough Castle can clearly be seen on the distant headland. Leave the field and join the lane by crossing over two stiles; turn right onto it. After just over ⅔ mile, at a road junction near a green, bear left.

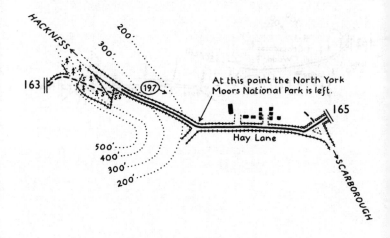

Walk past the church of St Laurence into the village of Scalby. Just inside the lychgate there is a wall plaque in memory of a courageous air-stewardess, Jane Harrison, who was awarded the George Cross posthumously in 1968.

SCALBY TO SCARBOROUGH (NORTH BAY)

The road sweeps round to the right, passing the Nag's Head Hotel on the right. On reaching the main Whitby–Scarborough road, cross straight over (with care) and follow the road ahead towards the A165; use the pavement for as long as it lasts, the grass verge thereafter.

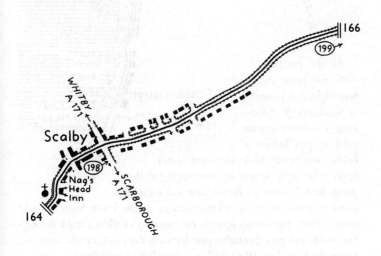

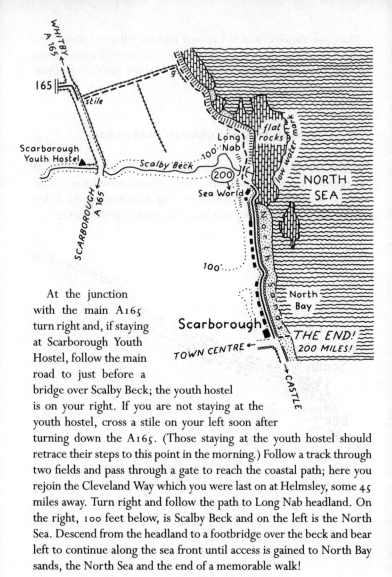

At the junction with the main A165 turn right and, if staying at Scarborough Youth Hostel, follow the main road to just before a bridge over Scalby Beck; the youth hostel is on your right. If you are not staying at the youth hostel, cross a stile on your left soon after turning down the A165. (Those staying at the youth hostel should retrace their steps to this point in the morning.) Follow a track through two fields and pass through a gate to reach the coastal path; here you rejoin the Cleveland Way which you were last on at Helmsley, some 45 miles away. Turn right and follow the path to Long Nab headland. On the right, 100 feet below, is Scalby Beck and on the left is the North Sea. Descend from the headland to a footbridge over the beck and bear left to continue along the sea front until access is gained to North Bay sands, the North Sea and the end of a memorable walk!

CONCLUSION

Over a number of years I have tried to understand what makes long-distance walking so enjoyable and memorable. Even before mapping this walk I had caught the bug having completed the Dales Way, Wainwright's Coast to Coast Walk and the Cumbria Way. Since this walk, I have completed three other long-distance walks and sections of a number of others. After completing Wainwright's Coast to Coast and this coast to coast I felt I was twenty-one again despite being twice that age! The hardest part of long-distance walking is taking the first step; after that you will should have much to remember.

I think long-distance walking, or even weekend walking, is a very different activity from a day out on the hills; it requires additional planning and effort but, as a result, the rewards are so much greater – none more than the affinity you gain of the landscape, and after 200 miles of walking you will truly be able to say you know the finest part of England.

During my walk there were some marvellous memories, and even moments of great spiritual uplifting. In particular, I will never forget the view from the edge of Harter Fell looking towards Upper Eskdale and the Scafell range where wisps of white cloud crowned the king of England's mountains, Scafell Pike. Later on, before leaving the Lake District, there was a splendid view of the Langdale Pikes and the waters of Windermere from Jenkin Crag as late afternoon sun bathed the area with its penetrating rays.

However, it was the arrival in Upper Dentdale which left a moving and everlasting impression. Always a secluded and tranquil valley, on this occasion it felt like paradise with the late afternoon sun, coupled with nearby sounds and aromas, touching senses which were heightened after 70 miles of glorious walking. I asked a local whether this was paradise and she agreed it was. Later on in the youth hostel I came across the following poem in a magazine – a sign that there are forces much greater than mankind?

Immobile Moors,
Ancient
Never changing
From age to age.

Yet ever changing
Moment to moment.

Sunshine, shadow,
Silvery rain
Fleeting over their vast beauty.

A tangible peace
Refreshing ourselves
World weary.

The silence
Sometimes splintered
By the trickling becks.

Paradise?
Not yet!
The best is yet to be
Our Birth into Eternity.

Anne Daniet

For some coast to coasters their 'Paradise' may simply be the 'Black Bull in Paradise' at the Theakston Brewery visitors' centre. However, for many the Lake District will have been 'Paradise' and Wordsworth in a few words enshrined its beauty for those with an 'eye to perceive and a heart to enjoy'.

'Tis the sense of majesty and beauty and repose, a blended holiness of earth and sky, something that makes this individual spot, this small abiding place of many men a termination and a last retreat, a centre come from where so ere you will, a hole without dependence or defect, made for itself and happy in itself, perfect contentment, unity in time.'

Another highlight of the walk was seeing snow-capped Ingleborough rising majestically aloof and condescending above the magnificent Ribblehead Viaduct. In Wensleydale, Hardraw Force and Aysgarth Falls were at their most impressive, bursting with energy and vitality after exceptionally heavy overnight rain. At Rollgate Bank, north-east of Helmsley, the North York Moors opened up their isolated and expansive beauty for the first time on the walk. The O.S. column should be treated with respect as I have adopted it and hope one day to have my ashes scattered there. Soon after, Farndale welcomed me with a fine yellow carpet of sun-soaked spring daffodils, clustered around the sparkling River Dove.

The sight of journey's end, Scarborough North Bay and the North Sea left me with mixed feelings of pride, joy and satisfaction at having devised and completed a long and beautiful walk, but also regret and sadness that a close association with the natural world had to end with a return to so-called civilisation.

You may well be surprised to learn that William Wordsworth has a little-known connection with the Scarborough area: in 1802 he married Mary Hutchinson who was born in Brompton, a village on the Pickering road just outside Scarborough. They were married in Brompton church and there is now a Wordsworth gallery nearby. Who better therefore than the great Lakeland poet to have the final word:

I heard a thousand blended notes,
Whilst in a grove I sat reclined,
In that sweet mood when pleasant thoughts
Bring sad thoughts to the mind.

To her fair works did Nature link
The human soul that through me ran;
And much it grieved my heart to think
What man has made of man.

Through primrose tufts, in that green bower
The periwinkle trailed its wreaths;
And 'tis my faith that every flower
Enjoys the air it breathes.

The birds around me hopped and played
Their thoughts I cannot measure
But the least motion which they made,
It seemed a thrill of pleasure.

The budding twigs spread out their fan,
To catch the breezy air;
And I must think, do all I can,
That there is pleasure there.

If this belief from heaven be sent,
If such be Nature's holy plan,
Have I not reason to lament
What man has made of man?

RECORD OF THE JOURNEY

	Miles Sections	Total	General Comments on Each Day
Day One			
Ravenglass	—	—	
Muncaster Castle	1¾	1¾	
Muncaster Fell	1½	3¼	
Silver Knott	1½	4¾	
King George IV Inn	1½	6¼	
Dalegarth Hall	1¾	8	
Boot	¾	8¾	
Eskdale Youth Hostel	1¼	10	
Day Two			
Penny Hill	1¼	11¼	
Foot of Harter Fell	1½	12¾	
Grassguards	1¼	14	
Seathwaite	2	16	
Walna Scar Pass	2	18	
Boo Tarn	1¾	19¾	
Coniston Youth Hostel	1¾	21½	
Day Three			
Low Yewdale	1½	23	
Tarn Hows	1	24	
Skelwith Bridge	4	28	
Lily Tarn	1¾	29¾	
Ambleside	1	30¾	
Jenkin Crag	1¼	32	
Windermere Youth Hostel	2	34	

| | Miles | | General Comments |
	Sections	Total	on Each Day
Day Four			
Far Orrest	1 ½	35 ½	
Orrest Head	1 ¼	36 ¾	
Windermere	¾	37 ½	
School Knott	1 ½	39	
Field Close	3 ½	42 ½	
Bowston	2 ½	45	
Burneside	1	46	
Day Five			
Oakbank	1 ¼	47 ¼	
Black Moss Tarn	2 ¼	49 ½	
Grayrigg Foot	2	51 ½	
Lambrigg Head	2	53 ½	
Lowgill	1 ¼	54 ¾	
Lincoln's Inn Bridge	3 ¼	58	
High Oaks	1	59	
Brigflatts	1	60	
Sedbergh	2	62	
Day Six			
Rash Bridge	2	64	
Ellers	2 ¼	66 ¼	
Dent	1 ½	67 ¾	
Tommy Bridge	1 ¾	69 ½	
Cowgill	2 ½	72	
Dentdale Youth Hostel	1 ½	73 ½	
Day Seven			
High Gayle	2 ½	76	
Cam End	2	78	
Dodd Fell	3	81	

	Miles		General Comments
	Sections	Total	on Each Day

Ten End	2	83	
Gaudy House	1¼	84¼	
Hawes Youth Hostel	1½	85¾	

Day Eight

Cam High Road	2¼	88	
Gill Edge	3¾	91¾	
Bainbridge	1	92¾	
Askrigg	1¼	94	
Nappa Mill	1¼	95¼	
Aysgarth	3¼	98½	
Aysgarth Falls Youth Hostel	½	99	

Day Nine

Hollins House	1	100	
Castle Bolton	2¼	102¼	
Redmire	1	103¼	
Wensley	3¼	106½	
Middleham	3¼	109¾	
Jervaulx Abbey	3¼	113	
Ellingstring Youth Hostel	2	115	

Day Ten

High Ellington	1½	116½	
Masham	3½	120	
Well	2½	122½	
Nosterfield	1½	124	
Ainderby Quernow	5¾	129¾	
Skipton-on-Swale	1¼	131	
Carlton Minniott	3	134	
Thirsk	2	136	

| | Miles | | General Comments |
	Sections	Total	on Each Day
Day Eleven			
Felixkirk	4	140	
Sutton Bank	5	145	
Cold Kirby	4¾	149¾	
Rievaulx Bridge	2½	152¼	
Helmsley	2¾	155	
Day Twelve			
Hasty Bank Farm	3½	158½	
Rollgate Bank	3	161½	
Dale End Bridge	2¾	165¾	
Lowna Bridge	1¼	167	
Hutton-le-Hole	1½	168½	
Day Thirteen			
Lastingham	2	170½	
Scugdale	2½	173	
Stape	4	177	
Levisham	4	181	
Lockton	1	182	
Day Fourteen			
Hole of Horcum	3	185	
Crosscliff viewpoint	4	189	
Langdale End	3½	192½	
Hackness	2½	195	
Scalby	3	198	
Scarborough	2	200	